The Library Administration Series

Lowell A. Martin, General Editor

1. Alex Ladenson, *Library Law and Legislation in the United States.*
2. R. Kathleen Molz, *Library Planning and Policy-Making*
3. Donald J. Sager, *Participatory Management in Libraries*
4. Betty J. Turock, *Evaluation for Library Managers*
5. Lowell A. Martin, *Organizational Structure of Libraries*
6. Norman Stevens, *Communication Throughout Library Organizations*
7. Tom Watson and Virginia S. Hill, *Library Personnel and Morale*
8. Ann E. Prentice, *Financial Planning for Libraries*
9. Raymond M. Holt, *Planning Library Buildings*
10. Sarah Leslie Wallace, *Public Relations and Marketing for Libraries*

The Scarecrow Press, Inc.
Metuchen, N.J., & London 1982

Library Law and Legislation in the United States

ALEX LADENSON

Scarecrow Library Administration Series No. 1

Library of Congress Cataloging in Publication Data

Ladenson, Alex, 1907–
Library law and legislation in the United States

(Scarecrow library administration series; no. 1)
Includes bibliographical references and index.
1. Library legislation—United States I. Title
II. Series
KF4315.L33 344.73'092 81-23176
ISBN 0-8108-1513-3 347.30492 AACR2

Manufactured in the United States of America

To Inez

CONTENTS

PREFACE

THIS *is the first in a projected series of books on library administration. Other volumes, to appear over the next two years, are as follows:*

Library Planning and Policy-Making
Participatory Management in Libraries
Evaluation for Library Managers
Organizational Structure of Libraries
Communication Throughout Library Organizations
Library Personnel and Morale
Financial Planning for Libraries
Library Building Planning
Public Relations and Marketing for Libraries

The series was instituted for a combination of reasons. The literature of library administration is fragmentary and in some cases out-of-date. Newer concepts of planning and evaluation have received only limited attention as they apply to library management. Methods for managerial control, such as performance measures and budget design, have not been brought into focus, with the result that many libraries follow administrative practices that are no longer effective. Insight that has been gained into human relations in the workplace has not been systematically incorporated into treatments of library operations. Finally, most discussions of library management are divided by separate attention to the different types of libraries—public, school, academic, special—without clear identification of underlying administrative principles.

Both the practitioner and the student have lacked a thorough and contemporary treatment of library administration. The series initiated by this book is intended to fill the gap.

It is appropriate to start the series with a volume on law and legislation. Although all libraries exist by legal authorization, direct or indirect, librarians are often vague about the law on which their agency stands. Administrators have enough to do with keeping their facility going and planning for its future. The legal foundation is often assumed rather than understood or examined.

Dr. Ladenson's presentation establishes the importance of the legal framework. He deals with constitutional, statutory, administrative, and case law, at the federal, state, and local levels, pulling all of these together into a systematic structure for libraries. From his extensive knowledge of the subject (he is the editor of American Library Laws*) Dr. Ladenson cites examples along the way from various jurisdictions. Where necessary for understanding, he traces the historical development of the legal framework. After an introductory statement, the several types of libraries are dealt with separately, and then together in legal matters that cut across type-of-library lines, such as interlibrary cooperation, copyright, security, and censorship.*

Running through this book is a recurring theme of the emerging federal–state–local legal structure of library service in the United States. The author presents this as well as the details of law in clear, straightforward language.

Dr. Ladenson is uniquely qualified for the task. He earned two law degrees from Northwestern University (including Doctor of Jurisprudence) and was admitted to the Illinois bar. He then went on to a Ph.D. in history at the University of Chicago. Dr. Ladenson held executive positions in the Chicago Public Library, becoming Chief Librarian in 1970. At present he is Legal Counsel and Executive Director of the Urban Libraries Council.

Lowell A. Martin
Series Editor

INTRODUCTION

THE term "library law" has at least three connotations, corresponding to the three basic areas of law in general: constitutional, statutory, and administrative.

Constitutional law as applied to the American system is the body of law that is to be found in the constitutions of the federal government and of the fifty states. A constitution is a written instrument that establishes, limits, and defines the fundamental powers of government and that distributes those powers among the branches of government for their safe and useful exercise. A constitution has been described as the highest expression of the law because it emanates from the people, who are the source of all power in this country. It is therefore superior to the will of the legislature, which, being created by the constitution, cannot change or alter any of the provisions in that document. This must be done by the people.

Statutory law consists of the compilations and codes of law that have been enacted by a legislative body. This body may be Congress, a state legislature, a county board of supervisors, a city council, a village or township board, or a town meeting. The acts of Congress or a state legislature are generally referred to as statutes; those of a city council or county board, as ordinances. Both of these constitute the statutory law.

Administrative law governs the functions of administrative agencies. Many of these agencies are authorized by statute to make rules and regulations, which—though they are sometimes called quasilegislation—have the binding effect of law. An example is the board of directors of a public library, which is an administrative agency clothed with the power of making rules and regulations governing the operation of the library. These have the effect of law, and to that extent the library board is a lawmaking body.

These three areas of the law are vitally affected by judicial decisions that interpret and construe the meaning not only of the provisions to be found in the federal and state constitutions but of the entire body of statutory and administrative law as well. As early as 1803, in the famous case of Marbury v. Madison (1 Cranch 137). Justice John Marshall proclaimed the doctrine of judicial supremacy. As a result of this doctrine the Supreme Court of the United States and the supreme courts of the fifty states pass on the constitutionality of legislation and are the final arbiters of the meaning of constitutional, statutory, and administrative laws.

The significant thing to remember about the doctrine of judicial supremacy is that the courts in the process of interpreting the law are at the same time *making* the law. Thus the declarations of courts often are more important than those of the legislature.

With this as a background, we can now define a library law as 1/ a provision in a constitution, 2/ a statute enacted by a legislative body, or 3/ a rule or regulation adopted by an administrative agency. Each of these legal instruments, however, is subject to judicial review and interpretation by the courts of last resort.

Because library law and legislation tend to follow the organizational patterns of libraries, I have presented the material in this volume for the most part by type of library: public, school, academic, and special. As much as possible I have tried to survey and evaluate the constitutional, statutory, and administrative provisions of the law that are peculiar to each type of library, together with the pertinent case law that is available. The book begins with the law and legislation that deal with public libraries exclusively and then proceeds to cover the other types of libraries in separate chapters. Readers interested only in school libraries, for example, can turn directly to Chapter VI. The final chapter, however, concerns special legal problems that affect all types of libraries in the same manner.

LIBRARY LAW AND LEGISLATION IN THE UNITED STATES

I THE HISTORY OF PUBLIC-LIBRARY LEGISLATION

To understand the law as it relates to the public library in America we must first trace its evolution. For our purposes it is sufficient to begin with the eighteenth century, when libraries were first organized in this country. The public library emerged as a legal entity in a series of steps from the colonial period up until the middle of the nineteenth century.

Proprietary and Subscription Libraries

Colonial libraries, of which the Library Company of Philadelphia founded by Benjamin Franklin is typical, were known as proprietary libraries. They were based on the joint-stock principle, in which membership conferred ownership of shares in the company. Shareholders were referred to as "proprietors," and the shares of stock were transferable by gift, will, or sale. The proprietary libraries were somewhat aristocratic in character and were designed to serve persons of social standing and financial means.

With the rise of Jacksonian democracy and the "era of the common man," another type of agency was introduced: the subscription library. To be eligible for membership in this type of institution required only the payment of an annual fee, or subscription. Many of these agencies were organized to assist young men who were seeking advancement in the world of commerce and industry, and were designed as mercantile, mechanics', or apprentices' libraries. Still others were established as part of the lyceum movement or as an adjunct to the debating and literary societies that flourished at the time.

These libraries, proprietary as well as subscription, were created as nonprofit corporations. In the colonial period they came into existence through the instrumentality of a special charter granted by the assembly and governor of the colony. After the founding of the federal government they were established by a special act of the state legislature, which had to be frequently amended to provide for changes in organization and management. Starting with New York in 1796 and Massachusetts in 1798, however, the states began to enact general laws for the incorporation of such libraries.

These early charters and laws enumerated the libraries' corporate powers, the most important of which were the following: 1/ to acquire and dispose of real and personal property; 2/ to obtain gifts, bequests, and subscriptions; 3/ to elect officers; 4/ to draft bylaws and adopt rules and regulations for the use and management of the library; 5/ to exercise the right of perpetual succession; and 6/ to sue and be sued. The administration of the library was entrusted to boards of trustees or directors, elected by the shareholders of the corporation or members of the association. Among the powers conferred upon library boards were appointment and dismissal of employees; fixing compensation of employees; purchasing books, equipment, and supplies; and arranging quarters for the library.

The legal pattern of the proprietary and subscription libraries left its imprint on the free tax-supported public library of today. At least two fundamental principles in modern public-library administration were derived from this early experience: first, that public libraries have an educational value and therefore merit the sanction of law; and second, that board management is a desirable form of public-library government.

The library of the eighteenth and early nineteenth centuries had a great deal in common with the public library of today, but there was one important difference: the early library was not tax-supported. To determine the origin of this feature of the modern public library, we must examine other phases of library development.

School-District Libraries

In 1835 the New York legislature enacted what may be considered the first state law providing for tax-supported library service. This act permitted school-district authorities to levy a tax for the purchase of library books. These books were intended for the use of the adult population as well as for students. The amount authorized by the statute was very small: $20 for the first year and $10 per year thereafter.

To assist and supplement this legislative scheme New York inaugurated the first state-aid program for libraries in this country through the annual distribution of $55,000 among school districts for the purchase of library books. The districts were required to match the contribution of the state. These early grants were made possible through federal funds that were distributed to the states under the Deposit Act of 1836 during the Jackson and Van Buren administrations. The national government found itself with a surplus of revenue, and it was proposed that these funds be turned over to the states. New York used its share for a variety of purposes, including the support of public libraries. This early fiscal arrangement therefore involved local, state, and federal moneys—a concept of funding libraries that is current today.

By 1847, with the added measure of state aid as an inducement, there were over eight thousand school-district public libraries in the state of New York with a total of 1,388,000 volumes at their disposal. Despite the rapid development of these libraries, the plan of public-library service through the school district began to decline, and by 1890 these agencies ceased to be public libraries and became school libraries exclusively.

The New York plan was adopted by many other states. Massachusetts, largely through the efforts of Horace Mann, organized about seven hundred school-district public libraries. Rhode Island, through the vigorous support of Henry Barnard, developed this type of library, which by 1849 practically covered the entire state. In Michigan school-district libraries multiplied rapidly as a result of a unique provision in the state constitution of 1835 (see page 14).

As in the case of New York, this form of library organization did not last in the other states where it was introduced, with the exception of Michigan, Ohio, and Indiana. In these states the idea survived to the present day, and a number of school-district public libraries are still to be found there.

The school-district venture in library service nevertheless established three concepts that helped form the basis for our present system of public libraries: the principle of taxation for public libraries, the principle of state aid for public libraries, and the principle that public libraries are educational agencies and extensions of the public-school system.

Another forerunner of the modern public library is to be found in nineteenth-century Indiana. The state's first constitution, adopted in 1816, authorized the establishment of "library companies" at each new county seat, to be supported by the proceeds of ten percent of the sale of town lots. The state passed a general law, based on this constitutional provision, permitting counties to establish libraries, the management of which was entrusted to library boards elected by the people in each county. The boards constituted corporate bodies and were granted broad powers of control. It was not until 1847 that provision was made for an annual appropriation by the county authorities, which was fixed at a maximum of $25. In 1852 the maximum was increased to $75. As a legal pattern of library organization these county libraries are merely of historical interest, for the county library as we know it today is based on entirely new legislation.

Emergence of the Tax-Supported Public Library

Prior to 1850 there were several isolated attempts by some New England towns to use public funds in one form or another for the support of public libraries. In 1810 the town of Salisbury, Connecticut, voted the sum of $100 for the purchase of books for a library that had been founded by a private benefactor in 1803. In 1827 Lexington, Massachusetts, voted at a town meeting to establish a juvenile library and authorized the expenditure of $60 for books and the services of a librarian. The collection was housed in the town church, and supplemental municipal appropriations were made from time to time. In 1833 the town of Peterborough, New Hampshire, organized a library and voted funds for its operation. Library service was carried on in a privately owned store that also housed the town post office. A board of three trustees managed the affairs of the library, and they were required to report annually to the town authorities on its condition. Peterborough lays claim to having established the first tax-supported municipal public library in this country. The library has enjoyed a continuous existence to the present day.

The year 1850 is a convenient date to mark the beginning of the modern tax-supported public-library movement in this country. By that date it was clear that the social libraries of the day were not adequate to serve the bibliographical and reading needs of the people. The time was ripe for organizing public-library service on a broader base. A number of social forces militated in favor of a wider distribution of books and information. The middle of the nineteenth century saw an awakening in the intellectual life of the people that was coupled with a more widespread interest in the arts and sciences. A considerable portion of the raw frontier had been subdued, and America could now turn its attention in a greater measure to cultural and literary pursuits. But the most pressing motivation for the expansion of public-library facilities came from the spread of free public education. The library leaders of that period came to regard free public libraries as an extension of the public-school system. Moreover, as municipal government developed it undertook to exercise authority over many functions related to the welfare of the inhabitants. By 1850 there emerged an unquestioned recognition that free public-library services was a proper function of city government.

We now turn to the first major tax-supported public library, the Boston Public, for a detailed analysis of the legislation that was involved in its founding. What occurred in Boston was significant not only because of its historical interest but also because it established principles that other municipalities were to follow.

As early as 1841 a suggestion was made to unite several of the library associations of the city of Boston into one free public library for all of its residents. Although this proposal was considered seriously, such a merger never materialized. In 1847 Boston received a gift of books from the city of Paris. Spurred on by this gesture of international exchange, the city council authorized a request to the state legislature for power to establish and maintain a library. (The Chicago Public Library also owes its origin to a substantial gift of books—these from Her Majesty Queen Victoria and the people of Great Britain following the catastrophic fire of 1871 that destroyed the city.) On March 18, 1848, the legislature of the Massachusetts Commonwealth passed a special law authorizing the city of Boston to establish a public library. The draft of the law was brief:

> The City of Boston is hereby authorized to establish and maintain a public library, for the use of the inhabitants of the said city; and the city council of the said city may, from time to time, make such rules and regulations, for the care and maintenance thereof, as they may deem proper; provided, however, that no appropriation for the said library shall exceed the sum of five thousand dollars in any one year.[1]

This statute was the first legal recognition by a state of the principle of tax-supported municipal-library service. The law, it should be noted, was permissive and not mandatory. It did not declare that Boston "shall" establish a public library but merely authorized the city to do so. Additionally, the legislature did not provide for the government of the library. It simply empowered the city council to make such rules and regulations as they deemed proper. Finally, it placed a ceiling on the amount of public funds that could be appropriated for the library. All of these provisions are significant, particularly the permissive character of the legislation.

Armed with this special act of the General Court of Massachusetts, the political and library leaders of Boston undertook seriously the task of organizing a public library. An important question that had to be answered was that of administration. Should the library be administered by an official, such as the head of a city department, who would be directly responsible to the mayor, or should some other scheme be devised? The matter was entrusted to a Joint Special Committee of the city council, which was made up of the mayor, seven members of the council, and five lay persons who were the library leaders of

Boston. As ten of the thirteen members of this committee were proprietors of the Boston Athenaeum, it is quite natural to presume that they used the latter as their model. The Athenaeum as a proprietary library was governed by a board of directors. Consequently the committee, with what appeared to be little hesitancy, recommended the adoption of the board form of government for the city library.

On October 14, 1852, the city council finally passed an ordinance providing that the library should be managed by a board of directors consisting of one alderman, one member of the Common Council, and five citizens chosen annually by a concurrent vote of the combined city council. The ordinance also provided that the board should have control over the expenditure of all library funds, should make rules and regulations for the use of the library, and should appoint subordinate officers and fix their compensation. The city council retained, however, the right to appoint, and fix the salary of, the chief librarian.

This ordinance, a precedent-setting event in the history of the American public library, served as an example in all sections of the country. Boston was the third-largest city in the nation, and the manner in which its library was to be governed carried weight. It was followed by one municipality after another.

To complete the Boston story, it may be of interest to note that the library board was made up of some distinguished trustees, including George Ticknor, a famous Harvard scholar, and Edward Everett, later to become governor and senator from the state of Massachusetts. These men were zealous in defending the interests of the library, and they fought to make it independent and free from the control of the city council. This desire to divorce the public library from politics originated here and has continued for over a century to be a guiding policy of library statesmanship.

Spread of the Public-Library Idea

Almost contemporaneously with the founding of the Boston Public Library similar events were occurring in other parts of

New England. In New Hampshire the first *general* public-library law was placed on the statute books on July 7, 1849. Its provisions deserve careful examination. The law was quite brief. The first section authorized towns and cities to establish public libraries and to appropriate funds for the following purposes: 1/ the purchase of books and other published materials, 2/ the acquisition of land and the erection of buildings, and 3/ the payment of salaries. The second section provided that the library should be open to the free use of every inhabitant subject to rules and regulations provided by the town or city. The third section authorized towns and cities to receive gifts and bequests for the establishment and improvement of public libraries. The final section provided that public libraries should be entitled to receive all state publications from the Secretary of State.

Two years later, on May 24, 1851, the Massachusetts legislature passed a general public library law that resembled the New Hampshire measure. It had, however, two additional provisions. It authorized the establishment of branches and provided for an annual tax not to exceed $1 per taxpayer for the establishment of the library and a sum not to exceed twenty-five cents for maintenance.

The New Hampshire and Massachusetts public-library laws, quite similar in substance, served as models for the other New England states. Maine adopted such a law in 1854, Vermont in 1865, Rhode Island in 1867, and Connecticut in 1869.

The next major step in the development of library legislation came with the passage of a general public-library law by the Illinois General Assembly on March 7, 1872. The Illinois Act of 1872 introduced a number of innovations in library legislation that are of considerable significance. First, it expressed the taxation formula in terms of a millage rate, with the result that library revenue automatically increases as the assessed valuation of property rises. It is of interest to compare this provision with the New Hampshire and Massachusetts laws. The New Hampshire statute merely authorized the municipal authorities to appropriate public funds without fixing any definite amount. The Massachusetts law specified a fixed amount per taxpayer. The Illinois law, however, permitted cities to levy a tax not to exceed one mill on each dollar of the assessed valuation of property.

Second, the law explicitly provided that the government of the library be vested in a board of nine directors, to be appointed by the mayor with the approval of the city council, and enumerated the powers to be exercised by the board. The New Hampshire and Massachusetts laws allowed the city and town authorities to determine the rules and regulations under which the library would be administered. Third, the Illinois statute declared that libraries could be organized in villages and townships as a result of a majority vote submitted to the electorate. The Illinois Public Library Act of 1872 was considered to be a comprehensive measure and served as a pattern for many states to follow.

From 1850 to 1890 the initiative for organizing tax-supported public libraries came almost exclusively from cities, towns, and villages. But in 1890 the state of Massachusetts enacted a law establishing a board of library commissioners whose purpose it was to encourage and assist in the development of public libraries. The act also authorized the library commission to distribute the sum of $100 to each new library for the purchase of books.

The library-commission movement, as it came to be designated, grew rapidly and was instrumental in involving state government directly in fostering and aiding the development of public libraries. New Hampshire adopted a law providing for the creation of a public-library commission in 1891, New York in 1892, Connecticut in 1893, Vermont in 1894, and Wisconsin in 1895. The Wisconsin measure became a model for many of the Midwestern and Western states. By 1922 thirty-eight states had made provisions for the establishment of library agencies. Although the government machinery for these agencies differed from one jurisdiction to another, their purposes and objectives were basically the same. The laws enacted for the creation of state library agencies were a clear indication that the state had finally come to recognize that it, too, had a responsibility in supporting the development of public libraries.

Up to 1900 public-library service was confined almost exclusively to cities and towns, even though at the turn of the century most people still lived in the countryside. As state library agencies were organized, however, they began to attack the problem of library extension, particularly to the vast unserved rural areas. County-library service was initiated and for a time was regarded as the panacea for achieving complete library coverage in every state.

California was the pioneer in this movement. Although not the first to do so, the state legislature enacted a county-library law in 1909 and again in 1911, which provided the legal machinery for California's present system. So well was the law drafted that it served as a model for other states.

With this brief history behind us, we can turn next to an examination of the legal basis of the institution that has come to be known throughout the world as the free public library.

II THE LEGAL BASIS OF PUBLIC-LIBRARY ORGANIZATION

To clarify the legal basis of public-library organization it will be helpful to recall a few basic facts about the nature of American government. Although reference is made to three levels—federal, state, and local—strictly speaking there are only two, for local government is an arm of state government. In the federal system political sovereignty is divided between the national and the fifty state governments. Under the Constitution of the United States, which is the fountainhead of all legal authority, the powers that have not been expressly delegated to the national government, or prohibited to the states, are reserved to the states or to the people. The Constitution is completely silent on the subject of cities, villages, towns, or even counties.

Cities and other municipal corporations, as well as townships and counties, are creatures of the state. The state creates them and the state can dissolve them, subject of course to constitutional limitation. Whatever legal power cities enjoy derives from the state. The United States Supreme Court has ruled that a municipal charter is not a contract between the municipal corporation and the state, and therefore it is not within the protection afforded by the constitutional provision prohibiting the passage of laws impairing the obligation of contracts. In Meriwether v. Garrett (102 U.S. 472) the Court declared:

> Municipal corporations are mere instrumentalities of the State for the more convenient administration of local government.

> Their powers are such as the Legislature may confer, and those may be enlarged, abridged, or entirely withdrawn at its pleasure.

Because a city or other agency of local government enjoys only such power as is granted to it by the state, it follows that in order for a city to provide public-library service on a tax-supported basis it must first obtain legislative authority from the state.

State Constitutions

As we have already seen, a state constitution is paramount to any law enacted by the legislature. Although twelve state constitutions have provisions relating to libraries, only two—those of Michigan and Missouri—have provisions that are of a general nature. Michigan's constitution has dealt with public libraries since 1835. Article VIII, Section 9, of the new Michigan constitution, adopted in 1962, reads as follows:

> The legislature shall provide by law for the establishment and support of public libraries which shall be available to all residents of the state under regulations adopted by the governing bodies thereof. All fines assessed and collected in the several counties, townships and cities for any breach of the penal laws shall be exclusively applied to the support of such public libraries, and county law libraries as provided by law.

This is extremely significant. The word "shall" imposes a mandatory responsibility upon the legislature to provide for the establishment and support of public libraries. Further, the statement that this agency "shall be available to all residents of the state" should be noted because it comes as close as we have to the legal mandating of public-library service. From the standpoint of sound and effective public-library organization, a constitutional provision such as this one is of course highly desirable.

Missouri's constitution also is of significance. It sanctions the principle of state aid for public libraries. This provision, Article 9, Section 10, reads:

> It is hereby declared to be the policy of the state to promote the establishment and development of free public libraries and to accept the obligation of their support by the state and its subdivisions and municipalities in such manner as may be provided by law. When any such subdivision or municipality supports a free library, the general assembly shall grant aid to such public library in such manner and in such amounts as may be provided by law.

In this case library service is not mandated, but once a public library is established the state of Missouri has an obligation under its constitution to "grant aid." Other states authorize financial aid by statute (an act of the legislature) rather than in the constitution (an act of the people).

The state constitutions of Arkansas and Oklahoma describe in detail how county and municipal libraries may be organized and prescribe the maximum tax rate that may be levied for library purposes. Such detail in the constitution is not a desirable practice, because the subject matter falls within the category of procedural details, such as the number of persons required to file a petition to establish a library or the millage tax rate to be levied. It is more practicable to incorporate these details into a general library law in the form of a statutory enactment. The constitution should be reserved for broad guiding principles of government administration. Furthermore, from the standpoint of efficient government operation, it is much easier to alter or repeal a legislative act than it is to change or remove a constitutional provision. The foundation should be in the constitution, where it will stand firm, but the superstructure should be authorized by legislative statutes, which can more readily be changed as circumstances demand.

There are provisions in the state constitutions that affect libraries without mentioning them directly. Examples are limitations upon cities and other agencies of local government relative to their taxing power and their bonded indebtedness, and to municipal home rule. It is also important to point out that state constitutions are redrafted periodically. When this occurs, librarians should take the opportunity to urge the adoption of a provision that sets forth the state's responsibility for the support and promotion of public libraries.

Statutory Law

The legal basis for most public libraries rests on a general public-library law enacted by the legislature of a state. Such a law authorizes the establishment of public libraries, provides for their maintenance and operation through taxation, and defines how they are to be governed.

Every state has one or more general public-library laws. In some jurisdictions these are grouped together in a separate chapter of the state statutes or the state code under the heading of "Libraries." In other states they are found in the municipal or educational code. One law may be framed so as to cover all types of public libraries, such as city, village, township, and county. Still others have a separate law for each of the local-government subdivisions. The state laws are similar in content and form, but no two are exactly alike.

What are the major provisions of a general public-library act? To begin with, it is not unusual for it to start with a declaration of policy relative to public libraries, focusing attention on the legal responsibility of the state to encourage and support their development. Section 1 of the Indiana Public Library Act of 1947 is typical:

> It is hereby declared to be the policy of the state as a part of its provision for public education to promote the establishment, maintenance and development of public library service for each of its various subdivisions. Such public library service is to be provided by a library supported by public funds for the benefit and free use of individuals and groups of all ages in the community in the meeting of their educational, informational and recreational interests and needs. These interests and needs are met by the collection and organization of books and other library materials and the dissemination of the knowledge contained therein through reference, loan and related services. . . .[2]

Such a declaration is more than an exercise in rhetoric. It has a direct bearing on the legal question of whether public-library service is a matter of interest to local government exclusively or to the state as well. The Indiana declaration links such service with education and states that it is to be for the free use of individuals. Both of these are vital concepts.

There are three key provisions in every general public-library law. First is the grant of power from the legislature to a municipality (city, village, township, or county) authorizing it to establish a public library. Some laws grant the power to the corporate authority, which can be the city council, the village board, or the county board of supervisors. Others provide for a referendum of the voters to determine whether a public library is to be established. Still others authorize the establishment of a public library through a petition addressed to the corporate body that has been signed by a given number or percentage of the legal residents.

A second key provision authorizes the corporate authority of the local government unit (*not* the public-library board) to levy taxes for library purposes. (In the case of a district library that is an independent government entity, however, the power to levy taxes is conferred on the district-library board.) This provision is generally formulated by one of two methods. Most of the state laws allow for a maximum property-tax rate for public-library purposes stated either in terms of so many mills on every dollar of assessed valuation or so many cents on every $100 of assessed valuation. In the remaining states the laws do not mention any fixed amounts.

The third major provision describes the plan of government for the public library, generally a board of directors of a specified number to be appointed by the corporate authorities or elected by the people for a specified term of years. The law also enumerates the powers and duties of the board.

In addition to these three provisions, almost every law contains a mandate that the library should be forever free to the inhabitants of the government unit, subject to such reasonable rules and regulations as the library board may adopt. Commonly the board is authorized to accept money, personal property, and real estate by gifts, by will, or through a trust for the benefit of the library. Also common is a provision authorizing the municipal authorities to fix suitable penalties for persons who injure library property or fail to return library materials.

The supplementary provisions relating to the library tax levy are vital. Some laws require that the proceeds from the library tax be deposited in a special fund (designated as the "Library Fund") and not be intermingled with the other funds of the municipal corporation. Others require that library taxes be *in addition* to all other municipal taxes or tax rates. For example, if a municipality is authorized to levy $3 on every $100 of assessed valuation of property, and also to levy twenty cents on every $100 for library service, then the total tax rate for the municipality will be $3.20.

In the area of library finance there are provisions that relate to the acquisition of land and the construction and repair of library buildings (including condemnation of property for library purposes), to the methods of funding such construction, and to the manner in which bond issues are to be floated.

A general public-library act can also contain provisions dealing with a variety of miscellaneous matters. The law, for example, can authorize the library board to extend the privilege of using the library to nonresidents under such terms and conditions as the board may prescribe. It can also require the board to submit an annual report to the corporate authority and the state library agency. It can make it possible to conduct a program of joint library service between two or more municipalities. Finally, the law can provide the manner in which a library may be dissolved.

The basic features of public-library government and administration are similar throughout the fifty states. Nevertheless, a close reading of the laws uncovers many variations. No two are exactly the same. It should also be pointed out that all of the statutes dealing with public-library service are merely permissive and not mandatory. In every case the law states that a municipality *may* establish a public library. Nowhere does one find that a municipality *must* do so.

There are other laws in addition to the general statutes that affect the administration of public libraries. For example, laws dealing with the form of local government, such as the city-manager or commission plans, can result in the partial or complete alteration of the method of governing the public library. Similarly, general laws relating to taxation, budget procedure, purchasing, and personnel have a direct bearing upon the operation of the library. State civil-service laws, too, have their application. These laws may or may not change the government structure of the library, but all of them influence its functioning.

City Charters and Home Rule

Another instrument that serves as the legal basis for the organization of many public libraries is the home-rule city charter.

The home-rule movement was born in the late nineteenth century as an attempt to grant cities, either by constitutional or legislative fiat, wider powers of self-government. From its inception in 1875 the movement has aimed primarily at freeing cities from irksome legislative control. This has been accomplished by legislatures conferring on cities the power to frame and adopt their own charters. The drafting of a city charter is to some extent comparable to the drafting of a state constitution. It is in the nature of an organic act, one that defines the powers of the municipality and prescribes in detail its form of government. The federal system and the home-rule idea have a good deal in common. Just as the federal system is an attempt to resolve the conflict between the national government and the states—in effect, a compromise between two sovereign forces—so home rule seeks to balance the powers of large metropolitan areas and state government.

City charters display a wide variety of library provisions. The National Municipal League at one time recommended that a charter merely cite library service as one of the functions that a city can supply. The organization of the library would thus be covered by a section in the charter that stipulates that all departments of the city government be established by ordinance. This approach allows the municipal structure to be as flexible as possible by giving the city council complete control over the details of local government. The charter of Pontiac, Michigan, for example, makes no mention of library service as a municipal function; nevertheless, the city has taken over the operation of the library under its general powers and administers it entirely without reference to the state library law. In several other cities the charter does not provide in detail for the organization of the library, with the result that its organization is defined strictly by ordinance.

It is more usual, however, for the city charter to describe the control and management of the library. Some charters have a clause mandating that the public library be organized and managed in accordance with the provisions of the general state library law. Other municipalities employ a slight variation of this legal device by providing that the state library law be applicable except as otherwise specified in the charter. In the case of San Bernardino, California, the charter merely repeats the provisions of the state library law.

But the more common practice in the framing of city charters is to draft new provisions for the organization and government of the library rather than to copy the old forms. As in the case of state library laws, there is no uniform pattern for the library article or section in city charters. In some charters the library article is brief, in others (that of Minneapolis, for example) it is quite extensive.

The home-rule movement has been a mixed blessing, as Howard Lee McBain, an expert on municipal and state government, points out:

> It is easy enough to say that cities may adopt charters for their "own government," or regulate their "municipal affairs," or exercise "all powers of local self government," but what do these undefined phrases mean? Who shall decide whether this or that specific matter is a proper subject for regulation and control by a municipality? And where a state law covers the same subject matter as a charter provision, who shall declare whether this matter is one of state or of local concern? It is the courts that have been saddled with the almost impossible duty of defining the vague and uncertain terms in which these constitutional grants of power have been made, and out of this situation a very considerable body of complicated case law has developed.[3]

Whether a particular government function is a subject of statewide or purely local interest is a complicated legal problem and one that the courts have been struggling with for decades. And it is not merely an academic question. The legal status of the public library depends on how the courts respond to this problem. It has come before the courts on a number of occasions, and judicial opinion appears to be divided. Let us first examine the decisions that hold that library service is basically a matter of local concern.

In an early Massachusetts case, Mount Hope Cemetery v.

Boston (158 Mass. 509), in which no library matter was directly involved, the state supreme court declared, by way of *obiter dictum*, that the city of Boston in operating its public library was not acting as "an agent of state government for the accomplishment of general public or political purposes," thus implying that library service is strictly a function of local government. In a somewhat later Florida case, Tampa v. Prince (63 Fla. 387), the state supreme court ruled that the establishment of the public library of Tampa was for a "municipal purpose." Finally, in a New Jersey case, Trustees of the Free Public Library of Newark v. Civil Service Commission of New Jersey (83 N.J.L. 196), the issue was whether the employees of the Newark Public Library were in the paid service of the state or of the city. The legislature had enacted a civil-service act covering city employees, and the trustees of the Newark Public Library claimed that they were not subject to the act because they were not a part of the city of Newark but were an independent legal entity created by the state and deriving its authority directly from the legislature. The court refused to accept this argument and ruled that the library is a municipal board and not an independent entity acting as an agent of state government.

Other court opinions hold that public-library service is a function of state government. A Michigan case, Attorney General *ex rel.* Macrae v. Thompson (168 Mich. 511), is one of the most important. The litigation involved the validity of certain bond issues of the city of Detroit that included those of the Detroit Library Commission. A lower court ruled that the bond issues were illegal because they were in excess of the two-percent limit of indebtedness restricted by the city charter. The attorneys for the Commission argued on appeal that it was a distinct and independent municipal corporation established for educational purposes, created by the legislature under its general power to maintain and enforce a free school system throughout the state. Counsel for the library argued further that the act establishing the Detroit Library Commission was not a part of the charter of the city and that therefore its bonds should not be included in computing the bonded indebtedness of the city for municipal purposes.

The question that was squarely before the court: Is the Detroit Library Commission, which is the governing authority of the Detroit Public Library, an independent corporation distinct from the municipal corporation of the city of Detroit to the extent that the two-percent limit did not apply to its bonds? The court's opinion declared:

> The act incorporating the Detroit Library Commission provides that its commissioners shall be elected by the members of the Board of Education. Both the constitution of 1850 and the new constitution of 1909 require the legislature to establish at least one library in each township and city. It is held that libraries are a recognized factor of civilization, a valuable instrumentality in education, that they enlarge and supplement the work of the schools, are within the proper range of school apparatus, and free public libraries are supplemental to, and a part of the educational system of the state. . . . Guided by the foregoing considerations, we are constrained to hold that . . . the library bonds . . . were not intended to be and are not included in the 2% limit of indebtedness for municipal purposes specified in the charter.

This is a very strong opinion in support of the proposition that library service is a function of state government. But before attempting to give it broad applicability to other state jurisdictions one must remember that Michigan has a provision in its constitution that requires the legislature to provide by law for the establishment and support of public libraries. Also, the Detroit Library Commission, because its members are appointed by the Board of Education, is closely linked to the school district of Detroit.

Another important case that supports the position that public-library service is a function of state government is State *ex rel.* Carpenter v. St. Louis (318 Mo. 870). This case arose out of the failure of the city of St. Louis in 1927 to levy a tax of two-fifths of a mill for library purposes, as required by a general state library law of 1885. The library board instituted a mandamus suit to compel the city to levey the tax. Attorneys for St. Louis argued that the operation of the public library was a matter of purely local concern over which the General Assembly had no control, and furthermore that the library act of 1885 under which the library was established was superseded by the home-rule charter for the city of St. Louis adopted in 1914. The issue before the court was clearly drawn.

In a lengthy decision the court began by declaring that the "general welfare" for which the state is responsible is a comprehensive phrase that includes education, and, further, that the public library is an educational institution. In language that was unmistakable the court went on to state:

> If a public museum (214 Mo. 231) is an educational institution in which the State is concerned and over which it may exercise control in St. Louis, then certainly a public library, *a fortiori*, is likewise an educational institution over which the state may exercise local control. That schools and their maintenance are separately provided for in the Constitution does not affect the question. Education is not limited to schools and it is within the control of the General Assembly, in the exercise of the State's police powers, to provide for other educational agencies. . . . As a State policy the General Assembly has assumed control of public free libraries as educational institutions. That is a legislative determination that they are a matter of State concern.

More recently, in 1945, the question under discussion came before the Supreme Court of Kentucky in the case of Board of Trustees of the Newport Public Library vs. the City of Newport (300 Ky. 125). In 1944 the General Assembly of Kentucky enacted a general library law that provided four methods for establishing public libraries. Upon the establishment of a library, the corporate authorites of the city were required under this act to levy a tax of not less than five cents nor more than fifteen cents on each $100 of assessed valuation. The city of Newport filed the suit questioning the validity of the statute. The question before the court was whether the General Assembly could require a municipality to levy a tax to support a public library owned and being operated by the municipality. The court stated:

> Having arrived at the conclusion that a public library is an educational institution, there remains the relatively simple task of placing it into its proper category in respect to local or public

> concern. . . . it is now recognized that education is a function of government. Such function or duty is not regarded as a local matter, but as a state governmental duty.

At the present time the question of whether public-library service is a local or state concern has lost its importance as a result of recent technological and societal developments. There is strong support today for the legal view that such service is a concern of all levels of government—local, state, and federal. In subsequent chapters there will be further reference to this question.

A complicated question affecting the legal basis of public libraries in Illinois has recently emerged as a result of the adoption of a new state constitution. The Illinois Constitution of 1970 in Article VII, Section 2, automatically converted all counties and municipalities with a population of more than twenty-five thousand into home-rule units of government and endowed them with extremely wide powers. A number of municipalities, including Chicago, Rockford, and Evanston, began to increase tax levies for public-library service, under their home-rule powers, beyond the limits that were fixed in the existing general public-library act. The County Clerk of Winnebago County refused to extend the levy requested by the city of Rockford on behalf of the Rockford Public Library, claiming that it violated the provision of the Illinois Local Library Act. The city thereupon filed a suit seeking to compel the County Clerk to extend the levy as requested. The case moved to the Supreme Court of Illinois, where a final opinion (75 2d Ill. 334) was rendered in favor of the city, holding that the provisions of the general public-library act were no longer applicable to a home-rule unit. The court declared:

> Formerly, the actions of local governmental units were limited to those powers which were expressly authorized, implied or essential in carrying out the legislature's grant of authority. Under the home-rule provisions of the 1970 constitution, however, the power of the General Assembly to limit the actions of home-rule units has been circumscribed and home-rule units have been constitutionally delegated greater autonomy in the determination of their government and affairs.

Another new development relating to the home-rule principle is the action of the Florida legislature in repealing its public-library act in 1973. This was intended to strengthen the home-rule powers of municipal governments. In adopting the Municipal Home Rule Powers Act of 1973 the legislature appended the following declaration:

> It is the legislative intent that the repeal of the foregoing chapters of Florida Statutes shall not be interpreted to limit or restrict the powers of municipal officials, but shall be interpreted as a recognition of constitutional powers. . . . It is, further, the legislative intent that municipalities shall continue to exercise all powers heretofore conferred on municipalities . . . , but shall hereafter exercise those powers at their own descretion, subject only to the terms and conditions which they choose to prescribe.[4]

The effect of this legislation is to transfer the power formerly exercised by the state to that of the municipality as provided in the Florida Constitution of 1968.

But what impact such an innovation may have on public libraries is not yet clear. It could result in undesirable consequences: the abolition of the library board, for example, or the loss of a separate tax levy for library purposes. It would therefore be well for the libraries concerned to persuade the corporate authorites of their municipalities to enact ordinances that contain provisions similar to those that were previously part of the public-library act. In this connection it may be of interest to call attention to the comment made by Carleton B. Joeckel, the foremost authority in the field of library government:

> The position of a library organized wholly under an ordinance, . . . is relatively very insecure as compared with one established under a state law or charter provision. Legally the library is at the mercy of the city council. At any time, the council, if it so desires, may repeal the existing ordinance and pass a new one entirely different in form.[5]

Although it is true that the city council can repeal an ordinance, it is also true that the law's very existence establishes a precedent, particularly if it has been in force for many years. A reckless act on the part of the city government to repeal it can be thwarted by an aroused citizenry.

It must be recognized, too, that a library ordinance is essential under certain circumstances. Often it gives effect to provisions contained in the general public-library act. For example, the state law authorizes municipalities to establish public libraries. But before such an institution can come into existence, the municipal authorities must pass an ordinance that confirms the establishment of the library as an official act. An ordinance is also necessary to provide the specific penalties for injury to library property or for failure to return library materials as authorized by the library act. In those jurisdictions in which the act is brief and merely authorizes the establishment of a library, an ordinance is required to spell out the necessary provisions relative to the government and management of the library. Finally, the fiscal operations of the library are based on an annual appropriation ordinance and (where a separate library tax is involved) on an annual tax-levy ordinance.

Still another instrument that serves as the legal basis of many public libraries is a special act of the legislature. Such a law is applicable only to the particular library named in the act. Often privately endowed public libraries were established in this manner in order to meet the prescribed conditions stipulated in a gift. Today there are still a few states that permit the passage of local or special legislation, but most prohibit it.

Before we leave this subject, we must give some attention to a group of public libraries the legal control of which is vested in a corporation or association completely separate from municipal government. These libraries are organized under a general state law authorizing the issuance of a corporate charter to educational and charitable institutions and organizations, including libraries. Frequently, however, there exists some form of contractual relationship between a corporation or association library and the municipality in which it functions. Where there is no written contract, there may be an informal understanding in the nature of a gentlemen's agreement between the corporation or association and the city government.

In summary, it may be concluded that the legal basis of public-library organization rests on a variety of official instruments, among them state constitutions, general acts of the legislature, home-rule municipal charters, municipal ordinances, special acts of the legislature, special corporate charters, and articles of incorporation.

III PUBLIC-LIBRARY GOVERNANCE

THE prevailing form of library government is the appointed or elected board composed of lay individuals. There are exceptions to this pattern, however, and these will be discussed later in the chapter.

Origin of Library Boards

The public-library board as a government agency owes its origin to three influences. In the first place it is the direct descendant of the library board that served as the governing authority of the proprietary and subscription libraries that flourished roughly between 1750 and 1850 (see page 3). When the Boston Public Library, the first major institution of its kind, was organized, it adopted the board form of management. The citizens responsible for its establishment were also active in the affairs of the Boston Athenaeum, which was a proprietary library, and it is natural that they should favor the method of library management with which they were familiar. The precedent established in Boston served as a model for libraries founded later.

The second reason for the adoption of the board plan of government for libraries was that public schools were governed by boards of education. This strengthened the belief that public libraries, which were viewed as part of the educational process, should likewise be governed by separate boards. To be sure, there are some basic distinctions between a board of education and a library board, and this may be the proper place to pause a moment to examine them. A board of education is responsible for the operation of a school district, which is a separate government unit or entity, of and by itself, established by the state with the power to levy taxes and to manage the educational facilities and necessary personnel to maintain the public schools. The school-district boundaries may or may not coincide with the political boundaries of a city, yet in either case the school district operates as a distinct and separate government body and is considered an agency of state government. In effect the state has delegated to the school district its legal responsibility to provide a common school education, which the state constitution has decreed.

The library board of a municipal library, on the other hand, does not have the power to levy taxes, for the library is not a separate government entity but a part of the municipal government that it serves. At most it is a department of the municipal administration. Although some courts have held, as we have seen, that library service is a function of the state because it is a part of the educational system of the state, the library board is not universally recognized as an agency of state government.

The third factor to influence the adoption of the board form of library government was the common practice in the second half of the nineteenth century of having an administrative board direct and supervise special municipal functions. Examples are boards of health, police boards, fire boards, boards of local improvement, city planning boards, and water boards. Summarizing this trend, a student of municipal government wrote:

> American cities have grown large and have rapidly increased and extended their functions. . . . The power to decide many important questions must be devolved upon someone and had better be delegated to a group of men rather than to a single individual. The group can gauge public opinion and public resources better than any individual; it can be made to include leading citizens as well as some specialists who are willing to give a little time to public service; it can have an unbroken life and follow out a definite line of development over a series of years. Its policy will be steadier, less fluctuating, than that of a series of single department heads. It will be more free from sinister politi-

> cal influences. It will serve through its membership to give many men and women a training in the responsibilities of citizenship, and it will serve to get a larger public acquainted with the work of the particular department. Finally, it is sometimes said that the board system saves the city money.[7]

Undoubtedly this trend of employing administrative boards in municipal government intensified the preference for library-board management.

The general term for the governing authority of a public library is "library board," but it is officially designated as the board of trustees, board of directors, library commission, or, as in Louisiana, board of control. Its members are referred to as trustees, directors, or commissioners. Municipal libraries governed by boards are to be found in every state of the union. Approximately ninety-five percent of the public libraries in the United States are governed by such lay boards.

Selection of Library Boards

The great majority of the boards are appointed by the governing body of the municipality, such as the city council, or by the mayor with the approval of the governing body. In a few states the general library law provides that the library board is to be appointed by the mayor alone without council confirmation. There are, however, a number of exceptions. A few cities use the device of the self-perpetuating board, commonly found in association and corporation libraries, in which the members appoint their own successors. This arrangement is generally employed by public libraries that were established under a gift or endowment from a donor who stipulated this method of appointing board members. Such a device removes the library board from control through municipal appointment and thus frees itself from the danger of local politics. But it runs the risk of failing to represent the community adequately and of withdrawing from the political process to such an extent as to endanger its ability to obtain sufficient public funds for the support of the library.

Another exception from the general pattern is the elective library board. The practice of electing board members is generally confined to towns, villages, and townships in Illinois, Michigan, and New England. The Illinois public-library act provides, for example, that library-board members must be elected in a special election on a separate ballot with the names of the candidates listed in the order in which the nominating petitions have been filed. The ballot may not designate any political party, platform, or political principle. The cost of conducting the election is to be borne by the incorporated town, village, or township and not by the library. Formerly library-board directors were elected at regular town, village, and township elections. But the law was changed when an attempt was made to have them run under party designation. A few large cities elect their library-board members, among them Grand Rapids, Michigan; Minneapolis; and Bridgeport and Waterbury, Connecticut. Most students of government frown upon the practice of electing such officials as library-board trustees because it enlarges the ballot to unmanageable proportions. Carleton Joeckel, however, noted that

> in spite of what has been said, it must be admitted that elected boards have been very successful . . . in Minneapolis and Grand Rapids. In both of these cities good men and women have been willing to run for the office of trustee and frequent re-election of members has been the rule. When a tradition of this sort has been established in a city, it seems unwise to change the existing form for theoretical reasons.[8]

Still another exception to the common practice of appointing library boards by the mayor and city council is to have them selected by some other government agency. In the case of district libraries, Indiana employs a plan involving three official bodies. Of the seven members of a library board, three are appointed by the circuit court of the county, two by the common council of the city, and two by the school board. In North Dakota and in a number of cities—Detroit, for example—the appointment of a municipal-library board is made by the board of education. This, however, does not make the library a school-district library.

The motivation behind this plan appears to be twofold: the desire to strengthen the library's role as an educational institution and the desire to secure an appointing authority that is less likely than the mayor or city council to be influenced by political considerations. But the wisdom of this procedure is to be questioned, for it results in diffused responsibility, with the appointing and the appropriating authority vested in two different official bodies.

Size and Composition of Library Boards

Membership on a library board usually varies from three to nine. Approximately twenty state library laws prefer five members. Another twenty states are equally divided between seven and nine. Professional library opinion appears to favor the smaller board of about five members. The only advantage of a nine-member board is that it permits wider community representation. In large cities this is an important consideration.

To bring the library into a closer relationship with the municipal administration some state library laws provide for ex officio membership. In an earlier day there was a fear that the city council might dominate the library board. Consequently in 1872, when Illinois adopted its famous general library law, it provided, and still does provide, that no more than one member of the city council can be appointed to the board. Nine states adopted this prohibition. Florida and Nebraska went so far as to prohibit the mayor or members of the city council from being appointed to the board. Tennessee went still farther: in that state *no* official or employee of the municipal government may serve on the board.

A later period has witnessed a reverse tendency. The New Jersey law, for example, provides that the mayor is to be a member of the library board—that is, an active member and not merely ex officio, and Louisiana and Kansas have made the mayor an ex officio member. Although it is quite apparent that a mayor might well be a powerful member of a library board, it is questionable whether a city's top official has the time for such an assignment. Nevertheless, in terms of contemporary standards of government, it certainly is not objectionable to have the mayor on the board in either capacity, active or ex officio.

Appointment of a member of the city council is not a widespread practice, but a number of city charters do provide for this. In Wisconsin, in cities under the commission form of government, one of the commissioners is an ex officio member on the library board. This plan deserves serious consideration. Such a representative can act as a liaison officer between the library board and the city council and thus dispel the charge of aloofness that is often leveled against the library administration.

In addition to the mayor or a member of the city council, there are very few other municipal officers who are ex officio members of library boards. It is curious that in Louisiana the president of the police jury may be an ex officio member in place of the mayor. In Minneapolis the president of the University of Minnesota is an ex officio member.

New Jersey and Wisconsin require the superintendent of schools to be an active member of the library board. The New Jersey act specifies that, if there is no superintendent of schools, the supervising principal must serve on the board; if a principal is not available, the appointment is to go to the president of the board of education. (North Dakota also permits one member of the board of education to serve on the library board.) The superintendent of schools is a desirable member, since the school and the library have a common purpose. A theoretical objection to such an arrangement is that the presence of the superintendent on the board may influence library policy to a deeper commitment toward service for students at the expense of service to adults.

State library laws prescribe relatively few conditions respecting the qualifications of board members. The Illinois library act of 1872 declared that board members must be "chosen from the citizens at large with reference to their fitness for such office." Obviously this is an extremely general specification and can be interpreted to mean almost anything. Seven states extract their wording directly from the Illinois statute.

With respect to the sex of board members, the library laws exhibit an interesting phenomenon: legislation is based on social conditions and tends to reflect changes in customs and mores. When women were struggling to achieve a place in the political sun, for example, a number of the state library laws provided that at least one of the board members must be a woman. As the battle for women's rights intensified, however, one begins to find such laws as the Ohio act that limits the number of women board members to three.

Two states, Oregon and Kentucky, have provisions in their library laws designed to prevent situations of conflict of interest from arising. The Oregon act prohibits any member of a library board from having financial interest either directly or indirectly in any contract to which the library is a party. The Kentucky law is even more stringent. It declares that no person is eligible to this office who is directly or indirectly interested in the sale of books, magazines, supplies, equipment, materials, fire insurance, or services for which library funds are expended. It also provides that no board shall employ as a member of its library staff any member of the board or any person related closer than a second cousin to any member of the board.

The matter of conflict of interest must not be dismissed lightly. When the library board is selecting a piece of property on which to erect a building, or when it is choosing a building contractor, it is the duty of any board member who has any interest in the outcome of the transaction, either directly or indirectly, to disclose the facts of the case and to request that he or she be excused from taking part in the debate and consideration of such matters.

To what extent politics enters into the appointment of library-board members cannot be easily determined. The Ohio library law provides, however, that no more than three persons of a six-member library board may belong to the same political party. Mayors select many board members, and it is likely that some will choose people known to them. This may result in the favoring of one or another political group. Certainly there have been instances of persons who have been active in a political campaign being subsequently appointed library trustees.

In selecting candidates for the library board the appointing authority, particularly in large cities, seeks to attain wide representation from the various segments of the community with or without political considerations in mind. There are usually representatives from business, labor, and the professions, from ethnic and minority groups, and from civic and cultural societies.

Some state library laws specify residence requirements for board members. Occasionally a problem arises when a prominent citizen is appointed to the library board of a city who happens to reside in a suburb. In such a case the residence requirement is often overlooked or the appointee uses a city business address. The New Jersey library law requires that four of the five board members be residents of the municipality.

The term of office of library trustees as provided in the state laws varies from three to six years. South Carolina stands alone in allowing a ten-year term of office. Most states prefer the three-year term, with the five-year and then the four-year term next in frequency. In self-perpetuating boards the tenure of office is usually for life. Practically all of the states make some provision for staggered terms, which allows for necessary continuity.

Automatic renewal of appointments appears to be a widespread practice, with the result that trustees are often retained long after they have ceased to be useful. Limiting the number of terms of a trustee can help to avoid this situation. But, on the other side of the coin, such a solution can prove to be a hardship, in the case of a highly qualified and dynamic person whom it might be desirable to continue in office beyond the period of limitation. The Utah public-library act limits a board member to two *successive* terms. This of course means that a director can be reappointed after being out of office for one term. This type of restriction merits wider acceptance.

Vacancies on library boards are filled in the same manner as original appointments. In elective boards the remaining directors fill vacancies until the next library election is held. Iowa and Indiana have the unique requirement that the absence of a trustee from six consecutive regular meetings, except in the case of illness or temporary absence from the city, renders the position vacant. This may be an effective device for removing habitual absentees.

Some state laws empower the appointing authority to remove any trustee for misconduct or neglect of duty. Such a general provision is susceptible to abuse. There have been instances in which entire boards have been removed because they have taken a certain stand involving intellectual freedom and the ALA bill of rights. It would seem only fair that the power to dismiss board members be subject to judicial review.

It is almost a universal practice for library trustees to serve without compensation. There are exceptions when a board member serves as secretary or treasurer. Many state laws forbid library trustees from receiving compensation, but some permit reimbursement for necessary expenses incurred in attending meetings. The time-honored tradition of service without compensation was broken when Los Angeles adopted a provision to its charter in 1925 allowing a $5-per-diem payment to library commissioners with a maximum of $50 per month. This innovation, it should be pointed out, was not instigated by the library commissioners. The framers of the city charter merely wanted to standardize provisions for all of the administrative boards of the city.

Joeckel's comment on this situation is interesting. He wrote:

> Even a single exception to long established custom in this respect is a matter of regret. There is little reason to doubt that adherence to the principle of voluntary service by library trustees has been an important factor in maintaining the generally high quality of membership which has prevailed. The introduction of a system of payment, even in small amounts, would no doubt make the position of trustee attractive to the wrong type of person. Worse still, would be the tendency to increase the number of meetings and to adopt a generally wrong attitude with respect to the proper functions of the board.[9]

Powers of Library Boards

As a broad principle the legal authority of the library board can be defined as the responsibility to manage the affairs of the library. But this concept needs to be examined in greater detail.

The board, for example, possesses considerable power over matters related to personnel. This includes not only the power of appointment but the authority to establish new positions, approve a job-classification scheme and salary schedule, make promotions from grade to grade, and dismiss unsatisfactory employees. In some jurisdictions the board cannot fix the salaries of the staff, because this power is vested in the corporate authority of the municipality. In such instances the board can recommend to the city council the rates of compensation for its consideration and approval.

Wherever municipal civil-service laws are applicable, however, the appointing power of the board is considerably curtailed. In weighing the merits and deficiencies of the civil-service system one finds a difference of opinion among librarians. There are those who believe that civil service has been responsible for saving the library from the intrusion of partisan or local politics or even board politics. It has also been a factor in helping to raise the level of library salaries by requiring all city agencies to adopt a uniform schedule. Other librarians have found civil service cumbersome and a drawback in recruiting competent personnel, particularly where rigid residence requirements are made a part of the system. It is also difficult to remove incompetent employees under civil-service administration.

The power of holding title to property as a general rule is vested in the municipality and not in the library board. In Chicago the city holds the title for the use of the library. There is considerable diversity of practice as to the power of a library board on its own initiative to purchase land and erect a building. Many boards do enjoy this privilege in their own right, while others are required to proceed in such matters through the intervention of the corporate authorites. In a number of cases this point is not specifically covered in the legal instruments under which the library is organized, and often the board is in doubt as to the limits of its authority.

Most library boards have the power of entering into leases for branches or other purposes independently without any action of the municipality. In a few jurisdictions, however, the board must obtain prior approval from the corporate authorities before executing necessary leases.

The issuing of bonds for the construction of library buildings is a power completely reserved for the corporate authorities and is not within the province of a library board. Where a referendum is required to float a bond issue, the library board is generally responsible for mobilizing community support in favor of the building campaign. In a few states the law provides for a separate tax levy for library-building purposes. Illinois, for example, authorizes the city of Chicago to levy such a tax. The library board submits to the city council an annual estimate of appropriations and tax levy for building purposes that includes new construction, remodeling, and rental of buildings.

Another question involving the acquisition of land for library construction is that of eminent domain. In Nebraska and New Jersey the library board itself is granted this right. Several other states expressly authorize municipalities to acquire property by condemnation upon the recommendation or certification of the library board. Most state laws relating to the exercise of eminent domain merely provide a municipality with the power to condemn property for public purposes: the library board must request the corporate authorities to take the necessary action.

A number of cases have involved the right of eminent domain as it relates to public libraries. In one Illinois case, City of Moline v. Greene (252 Ill. 475), the city proposed to condemn a strip of land belonging to the Moline Public Library for the widening of a street. The library board did not object to this action, but two local residents filed a suit to enjoin the city from condemning the property. The county court sustained the objection filed by the two citizens, and on appeal to the state supreme court the decision was affirmed. The court held that, even though the library board did not object, the residents of Moline had the right to intervene and question the validity of the condemnation proceedings.

In Hayford v. Bangor (102 Me. 340) the city of Bangor proceeded to take certain real estate under the right of eminent domain for the construction of a public-library building. The owner objected on the ground that the amount of land in question was in excess of what is reasonably required for a library building and, further, that the land was not suitable for a public library. But the Supreme Court of Maine upheld the action of the city and declared that: "courts have no power to reexamine the question of necessity or exigency, or the extent to which land may be taken for a public use."

Library Boards and Finance

The boards of municipal public libraries do not generally have the power to levy taxes. Yet there are those who believe that they, like boards of education, should have such power. But whether this is a desirable practice from a government viewpoint may well be questioned. Today the modern trend in public finance is to reduce the number of taxing units rather than to multiply them. In Illinois, for instance, there are approximately five thousand local-government units of all varieties, every one of which has the power to levy taxes. To add five hundred tax-levying library units to the already intricate government structure would doubtless lead to greater complications.

Although library boards do not enjoy the power of levying taxes, they do have an important role to play in the financial administration of public libraries: it is they who determine how the tax funds for library purposes are to be spent. The Illinois act of 1872 clearly provided that the library board "shall have the exclusive control of the expenditure of all moneys collected to the credit of the library fund." This has become a cardinal principle throughout the land.

In dealing with the subject of public-library finance one must keep in mind that the bulk of library revenue is obtained principally through one of two methods. One is a special tax on property usually expressed in terms of a millage rate, such as a fixed number of mills on every dollar of assessed valuation of property. The other is through a lump-sum appropriation from the general revenue of the municipality. Most states use the former method.

It should also be noted that the state laws contain provisions that either fix the minimum or the maximum tax rate or both that the corporate authority may levy for library purposes. Thus the Kentucky act, for example, provides that the tax rate for municipal libraries may not be less than five cents nor more than fifteen cents on each $100 of assessed valuation of property. The California law merely fixes a maximum tax rate by providing that the library levy shall not exceed two mills on every dollar of assessed valuation. Since most public libraries in this country are not operating at the maximum tax rate allowable by law, it is precisely in this area that the library board's role can make a difference. Often a dynamic board can persuade the city government to increase the library tax levy within the limitation fixed in the statute. In fact this responsibility constitutes one of the major functions of a library board.

The question of whether a library board can compel the corporate authorities to levy a tax at a rate that the board determines is necessary for the operation of a library has come before the courts in the case of Howe v. The Mayor and City Council of Des Moines (103 Iowa 76). In this case the board of trustees of the Des Moines Public Library fixed a tax rate for the purpose of maintaining the library and another tax rate as a sinking fund for the erection of a library building, and then certified both rates to the city council, all in accordance with the then-existing library act. The city council refused to levy the taxes as requested, and the board filed a suit to compel the council to make the levy. The attorney for the library contended that the statute authorized the library board to fix the amount of the tax levies, and that it was the duty of the city council to perform the ministerial act of actually voting the levies in the amounts as certified by the board. The lower court refused to issue a writ of mandamus, however, and the board entered an appeal to the Supreme Court of Iowa. The latter affirmed the ruling of the lower court, declaring:

> It may be admitted in the case before us that the board of library trustees is composed of high-minded honorable men and women, and it may be that this board is better qualified to know what such tax should be than is the city council. However that may be, the principle is wrong. . . . We hold that no officer and no board not elected by and immediately responsible to the people can be made the repository of such power. If this power was given to the city council and it was abused, the people could, at least prevent a recurrence of the wrong at the polls; but if it be reposed in a body not elected by the people the remedy is uncertain, indirect, and likely to be long delayed.

In another case, Datisman v. Gary Public Library (241 Ind. 83), a taxpayer brought a suit seeking an injunction to enjoin the Gary Public Library from taking any action to issue and sell bonds pursuant to the provisions of the Indiana library act of 1947. Under this act public libraries were permitted to reorganize themselves into separate library districts as independent municipal corporations with the power to levy taxes and issue bonds. The taxpayer contended that the library act was unconstitutional because it deprived the people of the district of their right of local self-government by permitting the appointment instead of the election of the board. The lower court ruled in favor of the library. In affirming the decision of the lower court the Supreme Court of Indiana declared that the legislature in its wisdom had the power to provide for the appointment of members of the library board, and this did not violate the people's right to self-government.

It is important to remember that there are two basic legal instruments involved in the government machinery that makes operating funds available. The *appropriation ordinance* is the legal authorization for the expenditure of public moneys and stipulates the amount, manner, and purpose of the various items of expenditure. The *tax-levy ordinance* is the formal imposition of the tax. Both ordinances are enacted annually by the city council or village, township, or county board. The form these ordinances take and the way they are initiated are of course covered in minute detail by state statutes. The appropriations for the library are included in the appropriation ordinance for the municipality. Similarly the library tax levy is a part of the tax-levy ordinance of the corporate body.

The library usually does not receive the full amount of the tax levy. From five to eight percent can be deducted for loss and cost involved in collecting the tax. A certain percentage of the property tax is never collected; there are always some delinquencies that account for part of the loss. In addition, the office responsible for collecting the property tax, usually the county collector, retains a portion of it to defray the expense of collection.

In some states there is a considerable lapse of time between the tax levy and the date when the taxes are due. In the intervening period tax-levying bodies are permitted, as in Illinois, to issue tax-anticipation warrants, not to exceed seventy-five percent of the levy on which the warrants are based. These warrants are sold to banks or government pension funds subject to the current interest charge. The warrants are redeemed when the taxes are collected and are payable only out of the proceeds of the tax levies on which they are based. When a library finds it necessary to resort to tax-anticipation warrants, its board authorizes the librarian or business manager to make the necessary arrangements with the proper municipal officer for the issuance and sale of the warrants.

Finally, tax objections are a vital concern. The law permits taxpayers to file objections against the taxes that are levied on their property. The objection may be based on an improper assessment or on legal flaws in the appropriation and tax-levy ordinances. When an objection is filed, the collector of taxes is required to withhold a certain portion of the tax revenues until the matter raised in the objection has been adjudicated. Unfortunately this process takes several years to complete. In the interim the tax-levying body is deprived of the portion of the funds that are being withheld to satisfy any judgments that may be rendered in favor of tax objectors.

With reference to budgeting, the library board is required to follow the procedures that the municipal authorities employ. Thus if the corporate body uses a performance-type budget the library board has no choice but to use this method also. There are three major steps in the adoption of a library budget: 1/ preparation of the budget by the top administrative staff of the library; 2/ review and approval by the library board; 3/ review and approval by the corporate authority. In the last step there is usually a hearing held at which the library officials are questioned and often required to justify their budget requests. Whether the appropriating authority will accept the budget requests of the library without revision depends on the relationship that the library board and the librarian have fostered in dealing with city hall.

Other Board Responsibilities and Procedures

Almost every board has the power to make rules and regulations for the use of the library. This is an important administrative power that has been delegated to the board by the legislature. It is under this power that the board is permitted to fix a schedule of overdue-book fines. Some of the state laws empower library boards to institute legal proceedings for the collection of fines and for the recovery of library materials. The board also can set fees for the use of the library for nonresidents. In recent years the question has arisen as to whether the board has the power to establish the payment of fees for making searches in computer data bases. In California the Attorney General ruled that fees may not be charged for this type of service. His opinion declared:

> The statutory prohibitions against the charging of fees by such libraries extends to all services that may be characterized as "library services," which in essence constitute the satisfaction, with library materials, of the patron's informational needs.[10]

Let us now review how the library board conducts its business. Meetings generally take place once a month, although some are more and others less frequent. In his study *The Public Library in the Political Process* Oliver Garceau recommended bimonthly meetings as sufficient to handle the amount of official business that a board is required to transact.

The officers of the board are usually president, vice-president, secretary, and (where necessary) treasurer. Often the director of the library serves as secretary. There is a growing practice to rotate the office of president, thus distributing responsibility and taking advantage of a spectrum of talent. The board functions largely through a number of standing committees, the most common being Personnel, Finance, and Buildings. It has become the practice for each committee to submit a report in writing with recommendations that the full board considers and adopts at the regular meeting. Some library boards are beginning to dispense with the use of standing committees and instead operate as a committee of the whole. As the board is essentially a policy-making body, this new trend appears to be more in keeping with modern administrative practice.

The board should not concern itself with administrative details at its meetings. This is the function of the director of the library and the director's subordinates. The board should concentrate on determining the policies for the library and providing for their implementation. The line between policy making and administration cannot be sharply drawn. However, the policy-making functions of the board should include:

1/ Making rules and regulations for the operation and management of the library, covering such matters as hours of service, schedule of fines, and nonresident service.
2/ Making provision for new buildings and their maintenance.
3/ Defining the library needs of the community in view of population shifts and other conditions of social change.
4/ Establishing public-relations programs.
5/ Making decisions on appropriate methods of extending services, including reciprocal borrowing arrangements with other libraries.
6/ Approving the procedures for the selection and purchase of all library materials.
7/ Establishing salary schedules and a position-classification plan.
8/ Providing for acceptance of gifts and naming of buildings.
9/ Providing for the welfare of employees.
10/ Assisting the director of the library in the preparation of the budget, approving it, and taking steps to obtain the necessary funds.
11/ Studying and supporting library legislation at the state and federal levels.
12/ Cooperating with other municipal officials and boards.
13/ Adopting bylaws for the government of the board, which should be in printed form and kept up-to-date.

School-District Libraries

In another form of public-library government the political unit is the school district, instead of city, village, or county. The school district, and not the municipality, establishes, maintains, and supports the public library. The school-district public library was one of the earliest forms of library organization developed in this country (see page 5). Governor De Witt Clinton of New York advocated in 1827 the establishment of a statewide system of such libraries. Almost a century later an important educator, Ellwood P. Cubberley, in formulating a utopian code for the mythical state of "Osceola," recommended that the county library should be administered under the control of the County Board of Education (and that the state library be operated by the State Board of Education). Political scientists, too, have nurtured the idea of a structural integration of the public library with the educational system. William H. Brett, a former librarian of the Cleveland Public and one of the library giants of a past era, harbored the belief that the public library should be organized legally as a part of the educational mechanism of government.

School-district public libraries are not school libraries serving students exclusively but public libraries required to serve the entire community. In fact some have no responsibility for the operation of school libraries at all. Another point to bear in mind is that the school district is a separate and distinct government entity even though its political boundaries may coincide with that of the city or other unit. It is a body created by the state to discharge the state's constitutional responsibility to provide for a statewide system of public education. As such the school district is a branch of state government and is no way subordinate to city, town, or village. This legal status of the school district has important implications for the library that it operates. As the provision for public education is a state function, the public libraries that are legally attached to school districts also become a concern of the state. Furthermore, because the district is an independent fiscal unit the library connected with it derives its funds from school rather than municipal coffers. Finally, the school-district public library is not affected in any way by changes in the form of municipal government.

School-district public libraries are concentrated in Ohio, Michigan, Indiana, and Delaware, with a sprinkling to be found in New York, Pennsylvania, West Virginia, and a handful of other states. The three largest are in Cleveland, Kansas City (Missouri), and Indianapolis, by those of Akron, Dayton, Toledo, Fort Wayne, South Bend, Terre Haute, Lansing, Kalamazoo, and Battle Creek.

From the standpoint of government administration, school-district public libraries fall into two classes: those governed by separate library boards appointed by the board of education and those managed directly by board of education itself. The former arrangement is to be found mostly in Ohio, and the government of these boards is provided for in a general state law. Each board of library trustees has seven members serving staggered seven-year terms; this allows for a new appointee each year. Except for appointment, the power of the board of education over the library board is almost nil. The library board is required to submit an annual report to the board of education—a rather routine matter. The board of education transmits the library budget to the County Budget Commission, but it may not make changes in it.

The trustees of a school-district library enjoy wide powers, like those of a board in control of a district public library established by law as an independent unit of government. In Ohio the school board and the school public-library board for all practical purposes act as separate political entities. This independence is reflected in the law that bars anyone from membership on the board of library trustees who is or has been for a year previous to appointment a member of the board of education making such an appointment.

It may be of interest to trace briefly the two reasons for the growth and development of school-district libraries in Ohio. One is relatively old and stems from the interest generated by the early New York experiment to which reference has been made (page 5). The other owes its origin to changes in Ohio's tax structure. The drastic limitation placed on the taxing power of cities made the financial position of municipal libraries very difficult. This situation came about as a result of the Smith One Percent Act in 1911, which mandated a severe limitation on the property tax. This legislation, one will recognize, is quite similar to the recent statewide tax limitations that have crippled public libraries in California and Massachusetts. Seeking a remedy for their plight, the libraries in Ohio explored other government relationships. Shortly thereafter the school-district library law was amended at the instigation of the Cleveland Public Library to provide that the library tax of 1.5 mills could be levied by the school district in addition to all other levies authorized by law. This move in effect placed the library tax outside of any limitations imposed on the school levy and assured the library of a tax rate of one and a half mills on every dollar of assessable property. Thus the school-district libraries prospered while the municipal libraries were impoverished. The result was a sizable shift from the municipal to the school-district type organization. By 1927 the number of school-district public libraries rose from thirty-three to one hundred and five.

This favorable situation for the Ohio libraries was of short duration. In 1931 a new tax limitation was passed in the form of a constitutional amendment placing a lid on all taxing authorities, school districts among them. The ensuing chaos was ameliorated by the adoption of a new scheme of taxation for certain government units, including libraries. A classified tax on intangible property, such as stocks, bonds, and other securities, was placed on the statute books, and this "intangibles tax" became the primary source of income for the public libraries of Ohio. Through the years it has proven to be a successful producer of library revenue. In the current urban crisis, however, the library boards of Cleveland and Columbus have found it necessary to resort to the property tax as a supplement to the intangibles tax.

Most school-district public libraries operate under the immediate jurisdiction of a board of education, including a large number in Michigan: Flint, Lansing, Kalamazoo, Muskegon, and Battle Creek are examples. Indiana has a considerable number, among them Indianapolis, Fort Wayne, and South Bend. The two largest libraries of this type are in Indianapolis and Kansas City, Missouri.

The school-district public library is linked very closely with the educational apparatus of government. It is thus integrated more completely into the educational system than a library controlled by a separate board. This arrangement affords the board of education an opportunity to formulate an educational policy that encompasses both the school and the library. Just what status this type of public library enjoys in relation to the board of education is not easy to define. It may possibly be described as a department of the school system. Of course some school-district public libraries of this category are sufficiently independent to require the use of a term other than "department." In dealing with library matters the board of education in some districts relies on a library committee that considers library business and refers it back to the full board for approval.

A common complaint of public-library officials is that the board of education does not generally devote enough time to library problems. Often library affairs are last on the agenda of a meeting and are pushed through hastily. One library has tried to avoid this difficulty by having library matters scheduled for first considerations at every alternate meeting.

This form of organization poses a delicate question with reference to the relationship of the director of the library vis-à-vis the superintendent of schools. Is the former an equal or a subordinate of the latter? In larger districts the library director usually reports directly to the board and in the smaller districts is considered a subordinate of the superintendent. Where the school chief is the administrative superior of the chief librarian, school-library service is likely to be favored over public-library service.

A library board usually makes staff appointements on the recommendation of the director. The fiscal operations of the library are closely related to those of the school system to the extent that the preparation of the library budget is the province of either a board committee, the school superintendent, or the treasurer of the school district. In some districts library appropriations are part of the general revenue of the school; in others the appropriations are based on a specific library tax levy.

An important question is whether the public library can be fused with the public school into a satisfactory whole. This writer is of the opinion that such an arrangement is not desirable. Although the broad objectives of the school and the library may be the same in essence, there are strong considerations that militate against such an amalgamation. The basic program of the schools is highly formalized and concerns children and youth primarily; the library's educational goals are cast in a loose and rather informal framework and are of direct interest to a clientelle that ranges from the preschool child to the senior citizen. It is difficult to unite into one government organization two public agencies whose everyday activities do not blend together with ease. Added to this is the fact that the methodology of the school and the library are not the same. Each requires a series of skills, facilities, and techniques that are quite different. For all of these reasons it would appear that independent administrative direction, for the school as well as for the public library, is to be preferred.

Other Forms of Library Government

A final area of public-library governance involves a large group of corporation and association libraries. These are managed by boards of directors in accordance with their corporate charters. The boards of corporation libraries may be self-perpetuating and membership may be for life. The boards of association libraries are elected by the members of the association for a given term of years. A few of these libraries make some provision for a limited degree of municipal representation on an ex officio basis. Generally the mayor or the superintendent of schools is designated as an ex officio member. This kind of library has a much larger number of board members than is the case in municipal libraries, with instances of as many as thirty-one members on one board. These people are often the most distinguished citizens of the community. The managing boards have exceedingly broad powers and owe direct responsibility to no authority higher than themselves. They are free to direct the affairs of the library in their own way and generally enjoy complete freedom from political interference.

In making staff appointments the board is not limited or circumscribed in any manner. The library is not subject to civil service even if the salaries of the employees are paid by the city. For example, an attempt to place the staff of the Enoch Pratt Free Library of Baltimore under civil service failed when the city realized that the library was a private corporation and could not be placed under civil service even if it wished the city to do so. The boards have the sole power to fix salaries, which need not conform to the municipal wage schedules.

The legal ownership of property involves numerous complicating factors. In most of these libraries the title to property is vested in the corporation or in the board that controls it. This includes buildings, land, equipment, and books. But there are many exceptions. In New York City the library as a corporation owns the superb book collections of the Reference Department, some branch buildings, and some special collections bought with corporate funds. The city owns the central building on Fifth Avenue with its equipment and most of the branch buildings with equipment and book stocks.

The income of the corporation or association libraries is derived partly from public funds and partly from endowments and other private sources. It is probably safe to conclude that in the case of most of the large libraries in this group the contribution from public funds exceeds manyfold the amount derived from endowments. Yet the conditions stipulated at the time of the original gift have crystallized into law, and the provisions under which the library is governed do not reflect the current situation. Although the city government and its inhabitants furnish the largest portion of the revenue for the support of the library, neither the city officials nor the people as a whole have any voice in the management of the library. As time goes on, however, and the contribution from the city government continues to overshadow the income derived from endowment, there may come a demand from the citizens that the library abandon its character as an independent corporation and agree to become a part of the municipal establishment.

Before concluding the analysis of public-library governance, we should briefly make reference to the position of the library board in municipalities that have adopted the city-manager or commission forms of government. Approximately eighteen hundred cities have adopted the former plan and two hundred and fifty have turned to the latter, but only a handful of these have made any significant changes in the legal structure of the library board. In very few cities have library boards been abolished. In Illinois, for example, the act authorizing the commission form of government merely contains a provision that the public library continue to be governed by the general state library law.

Evaluation of the Library Board

Turning to an evaluation of the library board as a government agency, one can make the observation that this branch of municipal government has been successful in attracting to its ranks men and women of extremely high caliber. In a study of the occupations of 638 library board members in 91 cities of over 30,000 population, Joeckel reported the following tabulation: 275, or 43 percent, were from the professions, with the legal profession furnishing 112 members of the group surveyed; 46, or 7 percent, were bankers or stockbrokers; 56, or 9 percent, were manufacturers; and 95, or 15 percent, were engaged in other types of business. The remaining 166, or 26 percent, were largely housewives, with a small number in the field of labor and government service. Even the severest critic of the board form of library management will agree that library trustees with their varied professional talents and wide business experience have contributed greatly to the development of library service in this country.

The board system has also been responsible for keeping unsavory politics out of the library. Rarely in the annals of librarianship does one find any serious defalcation of funds or political scandal. Library trustees have maintained high standards in making staff appointments. Though often under political pressure, board members have exhibited singular courage and independence in resisting this type of influence.

The board has also served as a testing ground for library policy and administration. In this context it is often asserted that the board of trustees is responsible for determining policy and not for administering the library, the latter being strictly the province of the chief librarian and staff. In actual practice, however, the librarian often initiates policy, with the board of trustees approving, modifying, or occasionally rejecting a proposal. Because the library administrator's plans and policies have to meet the critical eye and judgment of a group of intelligent laypeople, they are prepared with greater care and sometimes even abandoned because the ideas cannot be reduced to a satisfactory formulation. There is little doubt, too, that without the restraint that the board of trustees can supply, many library executives are likely to lose their perspective. It may be necessary at times to moderate the excessive zeal of the librarian with down-to-earth considerations, and this function a board is generally well equipped to perform.

The board also acts as an important instrument in interpreting the library and its problems to the community. In matters involving state legislation or action by the municipal authorities a prominent member of the library board can be of inestimable value. In the area of intellectual freedom the board can absorb a great deal of the emotion generated in such cases and deflect it in a tactful manner so that no permanent damage is done to the library or its book collection.

Turning the coin on the other side, one will observe that the board is also in an excellent position to interpret the community to the librarian. A group, based on a wider knowledge of the community, can feel the pulse of public opinion far better than a single individual. The board represents the diverse interests, as well as localities, of the city. Its members are usually old-time residents of the community and know its history and its people. They can help the librarian in many ways and prevent him or her from making mistakes.

There have been some theoretical objections to board management. Political scientists, for example, dislike the decentralization represented by the board. Moreover, they contend that it adds to the complexity of government and prevents complete administrative unity. Other critics have assailed the board system on the ground that it has not provided vigorous and dynamic leadership. They believe that the library, were it under the direct leadership of the mayor or village president, would have progressed farther than through board action. Boards have been criticized for attempting to administer the library instead of permitting the librarian to perform this function. They have also been condemned for failure to provide representation for young adults and for persons in the lower income strata.

Despite these objections there are those who are favorably disposed to the concept of library board government. William B. Munro, a political scientist of note, once pointed out:

> It has been suggested that in the larger cities unpaid library boards should be abolished and their functions transferred to a full-time, well-paid commissioner or director of libraries, but this idea has not gained much favor, nor does it deserve to do so. For among all branches of municipal administration the library department is the one that most appropriately lends itself to the board system of management.[11]

Finally, there is Joeckel's assessment: "As a governmental form the board system has suited the needs of the library admirably. . . . On its record the library board . . . has earned the right to survive."[12]

IV THE LEGAL STRUCTURE AND FUNCTION OF STATE LIBRARY AGENCIES

STATE libraries came into existence shortly after the establishment of this nation. They were intended primarily for the use of state officials and members of the legislature, but not exclusively so. New York, for example, in an act adopted April 21, 1818, referred to the state library that was being organized as a "public library" and declared that it was "for the use of the government and people of this state." However, the act also provided that no books could be taken out of the library for any purpose, thus restricting its use to reference. By 1840 the number of state libraries had reached twenty-two, and by 1876 every state and territory had a library at the seat of government to satisfy the bibliographic and information needs of its officials. The book collections in state libraries were predominantly in the field of law. But there were notable exceptions, such as the libraries of New York, Virginia, California, Massachusetts, and Illinois, which housed a considerable number of titles in history, economics, and biography. Like New York, several state libraries made their collections available for public use.

In 1890 there occurred an event that triggered a major expansion of the role of state government in the development and promotion of public libraries. Prior to that year state governments merely provided general laws enabling local governments to establish them. On May 28, 1890, however, the Massachusetts legislature adopted an act creating a state Board of Library Commissioners, whose duties were to help communities establish and improve public libraries. The board was also authorized to make a grant of $100 to any town without a public library, subject to matching funds by local authorities. The following year New Hampshire enacted a similar law, and in 1892 New York joined the movement by approving a comprehensive act in which the state library was designated as the central bureau for the extension of public-library services. As a result Melvil Dewey, who was then State Librarian of New York, introduced the concept of the traveling library. In 1893 Connecticut and in 1894 Vermont established library commissions like that of the Bay State: the free-library commission movement was born.

In 1895 this idea was taken up vigorously by Wisconsin and transmitted to many of the western states. By 1909 thirty-four states had created library commissions, boards, or similar bodies to stimulate the extension of free public libraries. Today every state in the Union has a library agency, created by law, whose responsibility it is to plan the state program of library development, conduct basic research on professional library problems, render consultative services to improve efficiency in library operations, and provide financial assistance to local public libraries as well as to library systems and networks.

It is worth noting that the development functions of state library agencies have not gone unchallenged. As recently as 1980 the Governor of New Hampshire proposed that all extension and consultative activities of the State Library be discontinued and that the Library limit its functions to serving the needs of state government. The proposal was not adopted, at least in part because of protests from the public, but the idea could reappear as financial pressures on government increase.

As other library needs arose in state government, they often became the responsibility of the state library. When state historical libraries, for example, were established, some jurisdictions placed them under the administration of the state library. This procedure was also followed in the case of legislative reference libraries and in the area of state archives and public-records management. When federal aid to public libraries was inaugurated in 1956, the state library was assigned the responsibility of administering the grants. Most recently many state libraries have become involved by law with coordinating cooperation among public, academic, school, and special libraries. The state libraries of today are multipurpose institutions charged with a variety of functions. A few state libraries, such as those of New York and New Jersey, perform practically all of the functions that have been enumerated, but every state library is required by law to perform at least several of them.

Legal Structure

In twenty-three states the management and control of the state library is vested either in a commission or in a board, with no substantive differences between these two forms of administration. These commissions or boards have from three to ten members; about half the states prefer a five-member board. Several states also provide for ex officio members, such as the state superintendent of public instruction, the chief justice of the state, or the director of the state university library.

Almost without exception the members are appointed by the governor, sometimes from lists of names submitted by the state library association. In several states the method of appointment is spelled out in great detail. In Indiana, for example, the governor selects one member and appoints four members one each upon the recommendation of the state's Library Trustees Association, Library Association, Historical Society, and Board of Education, respectively. In Mississippi two members are appointed from the state at large and two (one of whom must be a librarian) from a list of six names submitted by the Mississippi Library Association. The fifth member of the commission is the president of the Mississippi Federation of Women's Clubs or a member of the federation recommended by the president.

The term of office ranges from three to six years, with the five-year term being the most popular. As is the case with library trustees, there are few limitations on the number of terms that a member may serve. (Virginia restricts the number of terms to two.) Members serve without compensation, although the New

Mexico state library act stipulates that commission members be paid $15 per day while engaged in the performance of their official duties.

In seventeen states the library agency is lodged in the office of the Department of Public Instruction. It operates as a division of the Department and is governed by the state Board of Education in those jurisdictions where such a board exists. In Massachusetts the Division of Library Extension operates under the direction of the Board of Library Commissioners, which in turn is subject to the supervision and control of the state Board of Education. In New Jersey the state library is a division of the Department of Education and has an advisory council of eight members appointed by the governor to advise the state librarian on matters relating to the operation of the library. In New York the state library agency is under the Board of Regents of the University of the State of New York.

In Kentucky and Nevada the state librarian administers the library without the assistance of any commission or board. The librarian is appointed by, and is responsible to, the governor. In Florida and Illinois the state library resides in the office of the Secretary of State. The title of "state librarian" in Illinois is reserved for the Secretary of State, with the head of the state library agency given the title of "director." The Illinois law also provides for an Advisory Library Committee, which makes recommendations concerning the policies and management of the state library.

In recent years there has been a trend to reorganize and consolidate the administrative structure of state government. Louisiana, New Mexico, North Carolina, and South Dakota have lodged the state library in a newly created department generally designated the Department of Cultural Resources, which includes museums, art galleries, and similar institutions. Delaware and Utah have transferred the state library agency to yet another newly created depatment—the Department of Community Affairs and Economic Development. When these administrative reorganization schemes occur, it is important that the library agency be relocated to a department where it will not be buried or neglected. This writer is of the opinion that if the state library cannot enjoy an independent status, then an effort should be made to have it assigned to the Department of Education.

Functions of State Library Agencies

The laws describing the powers and duties of state library agencies vary considerably. A state library act often begins with a declaration of policy. The South Dakota act, for example, incorporates some of the most current concepts in the field of American librarianship. It reads as follows:

> The policy of the state of South Dakota shall be that:
> (1) Library services should be available widely throughout the state to bring within convenient reach of the people cultural, informational and educational resources essential to the improvement of their quality of life;
> (2) The provision and support of library services should be a necessary function of government at all levels;
> (3) The joint exercise of governmental powers under chapter 1-24 shall be encouraged where such action will increase the extent of library materials and services in a fair and equitable manner through cooperation between units of government and between and among libraries;
> (4) Cooperation among and between libraries shall be encouraged and promoted by the state library agency. . . .[13]

One of the primary functions of a state library agency, as provided by law, is to promote library service so that it is available to every citizen. This not only includes the improvement of public-library services but also extension to other types of libraries—school, academic, special, and institutional. In its mandate to promote library service the agency is also empowered to carry direct service to those citizens who are not served by existing libraries.

Another major function of a state library is to maintain, develop, and service a general library for the purpose of fulfilling the information and research needs of state government officials and employees. In addition, the state library agency in certain jurisdictions is also responsible for maintaining a separate law library for various departments of state government, including the Supreme Court. In New York the state medical library is also a part of the state library. Several state library agencies administer a legislative reference bureau, which provides assistance to officials drafting laws and publishes digests of current legislation. Some of the laws also require the library agency to maintain a historical library for the preservation and research use of materials dealing with the history of the state.

State library agencies perform a number of other important services. Some conduct archival and public-records management programs, covering storage and preservation, the disposition of records that are no longer needed, and the servicing of records so that they can be made available to the public on demand. Some state library agencies are assigned the duty of distributing documents to depository libraries. There are also some that administer a certification program for librarians.

State Financial Aid

A vital function of state library agencies, particularly in recent years, is the distribution of state aid to libraries. In 1835 New York adopted a law authorizing each school district to levy a tax for the establishment of a public-library collection. Three years later, in what Joeckel described as the first instance of state aid to public libraries, New York began an annual grant program. These early grants-in-aid were made possible through federal funds that were distributed to the states under the Deposit Act of 1836 during the Jackson and Van Buren administrations (see page 5). The federal government, finding itself with a surplus of funds in the latter years of the Jackson era, turned these funds over to the states. New York used the income for a variety of purposes, among them the support of public libraries. This early fiscal arrangement thus involved local, state, and federal funds. The present-day proposal that calls for a partnership of the three levels of government to furnish the necessary financial support for public libraries is thoroughly consistent with this early New York experiment.

In 1890 Massachusetts established a Board of Library Commissioners. With this came a modest program of state aid, one that was also adopted by ten of the New England and Middle Atlantic states. Annual grants were made available to each public library in a state for the purchase of library materials.

The economic depression of the 1930s forced local governments to look to the state for financial assistance. Ohio in 1935 and Michigan in 1937 enacted laws providing for the distribution of sizable amounts of state funds to public libraries. Michigan appropriated $375,000 for the year 1938. On a one-time basis Illinois in 1935 appropriated $600,000 to be distributed to every public library in the state for the purchase of books and other materials. Shortly thereafter Arkansas, Michigan, New Jersey, and Pennsylvania adopted new laws providing state-aid programs for the establishment of county and regional libraries.

In 1950 New York, ever the pioneer in the field of state aid for public libraries, introduced a most ambitious state-aid program, approving an act that would establish a network of cooperative public-library systems to be funded by the state. This was followed by another law, which established a companion statewide cooperative network, referred to as the "3-R" system, for the purpose of extending and improving the reference and research services for the people of New York (see page 85). This, too, is funded by the state and involves not only public but also academic, school, and special libraries. In recent years New York has extended the systems concept to school libraries. In support of these programs New York has consistently made large sums available, with recent appropriations totaling $35 million annually, or almost $2 per capita. Since 1960 the concept of the cooperative public-library system has spread to Pennsylvania, Massachusetts, Rhode Island, Maryland, New Jersey, Georgia, Illinois, California, Wisconsin, and Michigan. All of these states have appropriated relatively substantial amounts for the support of these systems. There are other states that authorized the establishment of these networks but have been rather slow to fund them.

The Urban Libraries Council, a national organization made

up of large-city public libraries, conducted a survey on state aid in 1980. The following is a summary of the data collected from the fifty state library agencies:

1/ Forty-six states provide some form of aid to public libraries. In 1980 Montana and North Dakota instituted state-aid programs for the first time.
2/ Thirty-six states provide direct aid to public libraries.
3/ Thirty-one states provide aid to public and multitype library systems and networks.
4/ Six states provide aid for construction of library buildings.
5/ The total amount appropriated in 1980 for all purposes of state aid to public libraries was $166,458,228, representing an increase of $12,344,352 over the previous year.
6/ This amount represents an average of eighty-two cents per capita for the entire country and an increase of five cents over the 1979 figure.
7/ The above amount also represents approximately thirteen percent of the total amount expended for public-library service in the United States.
8/ The largest amount appropriated by a state was $32,452,000, in New York.
9/ The largest per capita amount for state aid to public libraries was $3.61, in West Virginia. Next was Georgia with $2.47.

There are three fundamental kinds of state-aid programs for public libraries:

1/ Grants available to every public library that meets required standards.
2/ Grants to support the operation of cooperative public or multitype library systems and networks.
3/ Grants to assist in the construction of public-library buildings.

The formulas employed by the states for distributing aid vary widely. In some states the grants are based on the population served by a public library, coupled with compliance of minimum standards set by the state library agency. In Illinois, for example, the maximum amount of the state-aid grant is $1 per capita, but there is the further requirement that a municipality must levy a tax for public-library service at a rate that is no less than thirteen cents per $100 of assessed valuation. In New Jersey and Pennsylvania the amount of state aid varies with the tax rate that is levied by the local governments for public-library service. Maryland has a state-county matching state-aid program in which the minimum funding level needed to operate a public library is set at $6 per capita. A county that wishes to participate in this program must be responsible for at least sixty percent of the cost of the minimum program, and the state up to forty percent. Thus if the amount produced through local taxes is not less than $3.60 per capita the state pays the difference between $6 and the amount produced at the local level. In North Carolina, Ohio, and West Virginia state-aid grants are made under rules and regulations established by the state library agency. In Florida each public library is eligible to receive an operating state grant of up to twenty-five percent of the total amount expended by the library during the preceding fiscal year. Nonprofit corporation or association libraries are also eligible for this grant. However, no library may receive such a grant unless its operating budget is at least $20,000. The Georgia state-aid formula is based on the area as well as the population to be served by a public library, but it is also subject to the regulations and minimum requirements prescribed by the state Board of Education. In Kansas two-thirds of the appropriation for state-aid grants is distributed to public libraries on the basis of population; the other third is distributed equally to each of the regional libraries in the state. The Missouri formula is somewhat the same, but the allocated portions are fifty percent for local public libraries and fifty percent for county and regional libraries.

A significant development was the adoption of a law in which the state of Michigan assumed the entire funding of the central library of the Detroit Public Library, considering it to be a statewide resource facility. This step has relieved the beleagured city of Detroit from levying taxes for this purpose. On the same principle, that of designating a city library as a statewide resource, Maryland funds part of the operating costs of the Enoch Pratt Free Library in Baltimore. These measures constitute an extension of the state-aid principle that may well serve as a strong precedent for other states.

Although the recent statistical picture of state aid represents modest gains, when compared with state aid to public schools it leaves a great deal to be desired. State governments furnish forty-three percent of the funds that are expended in the United States for public schools, but only thirteen percent of those needed to operate public libraries. Over several decades the schools have moved from being funded almost exclusively by local property taxes to a position in which they receive an almost equal amount from state funds. If public libraries are to survive as vital institutions, they must move in the same direction.

To call attention to this problem the Urban Libraries Council commissioned a study on the role of state government in the funding of public-library service. The Council suggested the following areas to be examined:

1/ The legal basis on which state support of public libraries is grounded.
2/ The amount of financial support for which state government should be responsible.
3/ The formula by which state funds should be channeled to public libraries.
4/ The sources of revenue to be tapped for the funding of public libraries.
5/ The conditions that may be imposed on state-aid grants made available to public libraries.

The final report of this study, *Improving State Aid to Public Libraries,* was issued in January 1977 by the National Commission on Libraries and Information Science as a government document. The principal findings of the study are the following:

1/ There is a need and valid rationale for state government to increase aid to public libraries.
2/ The fiscal condition of many of the states is such that

permits them to assume a greater proportion of the financial support of public libraries.

3/ Library expenditures have not kept pace with similar public expenditures or with inflation.

4/ The historical development and growth of public education and public libraries are parallel and represent a comparable response to the same societal needs for education and knowledge.

5/ Public libraries have felt the effects of the fiscal crunch more than most local services, because, more than most functions, they have depended on local revenue resources for their funding.

An earlier survey, *Alternatives for Financing the Public Library,* also published by the National Commission on Libraries and Information Science as a public document, recommended a balanced intergovernmental pattern for funding public libraries to be achieved over a period of ten years. The final formula would require the state to be responsible for fifty percent, local government for thirty percent, and the federal government for twenty percent of the amount needed to operate and maintain the public libraries of this country.

In 1963 *Standards for Library Functions at the State Level,* published by the American Library Association, proposed that "the state share in the financing of local public library service should be at least one third to one half of the total cost of a sound minimum library program as set forth in the state plan for library development."[14]

There are two reasons for making fundamental changes in the current legal provisions for financing public libraries. The first is due to the drawbacks of the local property tax, upon which public libraries are primarily dependent. This tax is a highly regressive one and, moreover, lacks elasticity. Unlike the income and sales taxes, which generate additional revenue automatically as wages and prices rise, the revenue from the property tax remains relatively constant, increasing only gradually with the total assessed valuation of property. This is particularly disastrous in periods of high inflation, such as this country has witnessed now for almost a decade.

To make matters worse, the property tax is now under serious attack by those who seek indiscriminately to limit government expenditures. It began in earnest with Proposition 13 in California and has spread to other jurisdictions. This has been a tremendous blow to many public libraries throughout the land, for they are extremely vulnerable when budgets are to be slashed. Everywhere librarians are hearing the cry of austerity. It is something of a miracle that Proposition 9, designed to cut the state income tax, was defeated by the voters of California in June 1980. But the philosophy of Howard Jarvis will not lie dormant. It is certain to reappear again and again.

A second problem that makes it imperative to alter the present scheme of funding public libraries is the flood of lawsuits seeking to invalidate the present system of financing public education. The most celebrated case is Serrano v. Priest (5 Cal. 3d 584), decided in 1971 by the California Supreme Court. In this suit the plaintiffs charged that the public-school system in California is based on revenue that depends largely on funds derived from local property taxes and that this method results in gross disparities between individual school districts in the amount of money available per pupil. Districts with small tax bases are not able to provide as much money per child as districts with large assessed valuations of property. Thus the educational opportunities made available in the district where the children of the plaintiffs reside are considerably inferior to those made available to children attending schools in many of the other districts in the state. The plaintiffs therefore argued that the California financing scheme for public education fails to meet the requirements of the equal-protection clause of the Fourteenth Amendment of the U.S. Constitution and is also in conflict with provisions of the California Constitution.

In a landmark decision the court held for the plaintiffs. Justice Sullivan's opinion included the following paragraph:

> We are called upon to determine whether the California public school financing system, with its substantial dependence on local property taxes and resultant wide disparities in school revenue, violates the equal protection clause of the Fourteenth Amendment. We have determined that this funding scheme

> invidiously discriminates against the poor because it makes the quality of a child's education a function of the wealth of the parents and neighbors. Recognizing as we must that the right to an education in our public schools is a fundamental interest which cannot be conditioned on wealth, we can discern no compelling state purpose necessitating the present method of financing. We have concluded, therefore, that such a system cannot withstand constitutional challenge and must fall before the equal protection clause.

In 1972, one year after the *Serrano* decision, the same legal issues were presented to the U.S. Supreme Court in the case of San Antonio Independent School District v. Rodriguez (411 U.S. 1). The facts in this case are substantially the same as in *Serrano*. However, by a five-to-four decision the Supreme Court held that the financing scheme of public education in the state of Texas did not constitute a violation of the equal-protection clause of the Fourteenth Amendment. Justice Powell, writing for the majority, declared:

> The consideration and initiation of fundamental reforms with respect to state taxation and education are matters reserved for the legislative processes of the various States. . . . We hardly need add that this Court's action today is not to be viewed as placing its judicial imprimatur on the status quo. The need is apparent for reform in tax systems which may well have relied too long and too heavily on the local property tax. And certainly innovative thinking as to public education, its methods, and its funding is necessary to assure both a higher level of quality and greater uniformity of opportunity. These matters merit the continued attention of the scholars who already have contributed much by their challenges. But the ultimate solutions must come from the lawmakers and from the democratic pressures of those who elect them.

Justice Marshall, with whom Justice Douglas concurred, wrote a strong dissenting opinion in which he stated:

> The Court today decides, in effect, that a State may constitutionally vary the quality of education which it offers its children in accordance with the amount of taxable wealth located in the

> school districts within which they reside. The majority's decision represents an abrupt departure from the mainstream of recent state and federal court decisions concerning the unconstitutionality of state educational financing schemes dependent upon taxable local wealth. More unfortunately, though, the majority's holding can only be seen as a retreat from our historic commitment to equality of educational opportunity and as unsupportable acquiescence in a system which deprives children in their earliest years of the chance to reach their full potential as citizens. The court does this despite the absence of any substantial justification for a scheme which arbitrarily channels educational resources in accordance with the fortuity of the amount of taxable wealth within each district.

The *Rodriguez* decision is diametrically opposed to the *Serrano* decision, but the ruling of the U.S. Supreme Court takes precedence over the ruling of a state court: *Rodriguez* is now the law of the land. Yet one must keep in mind that *Rodriguez* was a close decision, five to four, and if social conditions change, it could be overturned at some future date. Additionally, the two courts differed only on the fundamental question of whether there was an infraction of the equal-protection clause. Both agreed that the present system of funding public education, which produces serious disparities in the amount of per-pupil revenue available for education, needs to be remedied. (Justice Stewart, concurring with the majority, wrote a separate opinion in which he noted that "the method of financing public schools in Texas, as in almost every other State, has resulted in a system of public education that can be fairly described as chaotic and unjust.") *Rodriguez*, however, insists that the state legislature must apply the remedy; *Serrano*, that it is the function of the court to prod the legislature into action.

It is quite clear that the use of the local property tax to finance public education will continue to be under attack. In New Jersey, for example, the legislature recently imposed a state income tax to bail out the beleaguered school districts that depended so heavily on the local property tax. This action was no doubt influenced by the 1973 decision in Robinson v. Cahill (62 N.J. 473), in which the New Jersey Supreme Court held unanimously that the public-school financing system was unconstitutional, not under the Fourteenth Amendment but under a provision of the state constitution that required "the maintenance and support of a thorough and efficient system of free public schools." There have been similar lawsuits in Michigan, Minnesota, and New York.

The issues raised in *Rodriguez* and *Serrano* have important implications for public libraries. There are gross disparities in the amount of property-tax revenue available for library service among a state's local-government units. The supreme courts of no fewer than nine states[15] have declared public libraries to be educational institutions, and each state should be responsible for ensuring equality of library service among its citizens. The only practical way to eliminate these disparities is to inject large doses of state aid.

It is becoming increasingly clear that there is nothing in law, logic, or public policy that dictates that public libraries must be financed chiefly through local funds. The recommendation of the NCLIS report referred to above, declaring that the states should provide fifty percent of the cost of operating the nation's public libraries, is not only reasonable but also attainable over a period of years. It is up to librarians and trustees to mobilize support for achieving such a goal.

Interstate Compacts

Thirty-two states have adopted the interstate library compact in one form or another. This legal device has been employed for a number of years to make possible joint action between neighboring state governments, thus extending the principle of library cooperation and consolidation across state lines.

The document setting forth provisions for interstate action usually begins with a statement of policy and purpose, of which the following, from New York state, is a typical example:

> Because the desire for the services provided by the libraries transcends governmental boundaries and can most effectively

> be satisfied by giving such services to communities and people regardless of jurisdictional lines, it is the policy of the states party to this compact to cooperate and share their responsibilities; to authorize cooperation and sharing with respect to those types of library facilities and services which can be more economically or efficiently developed and maintained on a cooperative basis, and to authorize cooperation and sharing among localities, states and others in providing joint or cooperative library services in areas where the distribution of population or of existing and potential library resources make the provision of library service on an interstate basis the most effective way of providing adequate and efficient service.[16]

The interstate compact authorizes one or more libraries within a state, usually public libraries, to enter into an agreement with one or more libraries in another state and establishes an interstate library district, seemed to be a separate corporate body. Within this district—which is governed by a board made up of representatives of member libraries—library functions may be undertaken on a joint or cooperative basis or by means of other arrangements as provided in the agreement between the contracting parties.

The agreement sets forth the services, programs, and facilities that the district is to undertake. It provides for the allocation of costs and other financial responsibilities and specifies the respective rights, duties, obligations, and liabilities of the contracting parties. The agreement does not become effective until it is filed with the compact administrator of each state and approved by the respective attorneys-general. In many jurisdictions the state librarian is designated the compact administrator.

The compact permits any public library to appropriate funds to the interstate library district in the same manner as its own appropriations are made. It also permits such a district to claim and receive state and federal aid.

Although thirty-two states have adopted the interstate library compact, there has been relatively little use made of it. However, as more multitype library cooperative projects are organized on a regional basis, this legal technique may be employed more widely in the future.

Certification of Librarians

Twenty-one states have statutory enactments of one kind or another dealing with certification of library personnel. Some of the laws are brief, merely authorizing the state library agency to make rules and regulations for the purpose. Other laws are comprehensive. The Kentucky statute is applicable to all libraries supported with public funds, with the exception of law and legislative reference libraries, school libraries, and libraries serving government units having a population of less than three thousand.

The Kentucky law, as one example, provides for the establishment of a certification board within the Department of Libraries and Archives. The board consists of the director of the latter department and five members appointed by the governor from a list submitted by the Kentucky Library Association. Two members must be full-time professional librarians actively engaged in the public-library field. Two members must be public-library trustees and the fifth member a professional librarian from a department or school of library science in a state university. The term of office for board members is four years, and the board is required to hold at least one meeting per year with such special meetings as are necessary. Members receive $25 per day for each meeting they attend plus expenses.

The board has the power to issue certificates of librarianship without examination to applicants who are graduates of library schools approved by the board. It can certify other applicants when it has satisfied itself by examination that they are qualified for professional library work. It has the authority to renew certificates and to adopt rules and regulations for its own government. The board is required to hold hearings to reconsider applications that it has rejected. The law provides for a court with competent jurisdiction to review decisions involving the refusal to issue a certificate. The so-called "grandfather clause" entitles librarians in service as of a given date to receive a life certificate without examination.

The law forbids libraries, subject to the provisions of the act, from employing any person in a full-time professional position who does not hold a certificate of librarianship issued by the board. It also sets out penalties for the violation of any provisions of the act. The Kentucky statute is an example of certification in detail and with provision for enforcement. Many states have less formal arrangements, without legal force, that are voluntary on the part of both practitioners and employing agencies. In some such cases the regulations have become practically inoperative.

It is safe to predict that, in the years ahead, the functions of state library agencies will continue to be augmented, this for three reasons: 1/ they will be in the forefront in initiating and coordinating cooperative multitype library networks; 2/ possible increases in federal aid will continue to be channeled through these agencies; and 3/ increased state aid to public libraries will provide them with greater opportunities for improving and equalizing library service for every citizen.

V THE LEGAL ORGANIZATION OF PUBLIC AND MULTITYPE LIBRARY SYSTEMS AND NETWORKS

FROM 1850 to the turn of the century the free-public-library movement was for the most part an urban phenomenon. Service was confined almost exclusively to city dwellers, notwithstanding the larger number of rural Americans. As the twentieth century opened, however, librarians began to explore ways to reach this vast unserved population. The state library commissions, the first to attack the problem, soon realized that if universal library service was to be achieved, the unit of government that provided it would have to be enlarged. Now, the *county* would become responsible for extending library service to those areas where it did not exist.

County Libraries

Although county libraries today are found in most of the states, they are concentrated in the South and Far West. From the standpoint of government organization, there are three types: 1/ libraries that are part of county government; 2/ libraries that are part of both city and county governments; and 3/ municipal libraries that serve the county by contract. Some libraries serve the entire county and some serve only a portion of it, usually omitting those municipalities that operate libraries independently.

California was one of the pioneer states to adopt the county-library form of organization. Under California law a county board of supervisors exercises the same powers over the library as a board of trustees does over a municipal library. The board is authorized to establish a free library for that portion of the county lying outside of cities that maintain free public libraries and districts that maintain district libraries. Any city or district library may become part of the county system by making the property within the city or district subject to taxes levied for county-library purposes. The board of supervisors also can contract to furnish library service to another county. Where it is not feasible to establish a separate county library, the board may contract with a city library to assume the functions of one.

In its legal structure the county library is a department of county government. The board of supervisors appoints the county librarian, who must have received a certificate of qualification from the board of library examiners. This board, chaired ex officio by the state librarian, is made up of the librarians of the city and county of San Francisco and of the Los Angeles Public Library. The board of supervisors levies a library tax annually in the same manner and at the same time as other county taxes.

California maintains a certain degree of control over county libraries by placing them under the supervision of the state librarian, who visits or sends assistants to the libraries from time to time and inquires into their condition. This unique provision appears to be borrowed from the school code.

The county libraries of California have also been successful in bringing under their jurisdiction a high proportion of the school libraries of the state. Under the law the board of supervisors may accept books and other property of school and teachers' libraries and manage and operate them as a part of the county collection. This amalgamation of service has helped the growth of the county-library movement in the state.

Furthermore, the law provides that the board of supervisors may contract with the trustees of a county law library to assume the functions of the law library; compensation is paid into the county-library fund. Each board of supervisors is also authorized to extend library service to charitable, detention, and penal institutions and to provide library service to county officials and employees.

The county-library system has flourished in California with the result that much, if not all, of the state has good library service. This system is now being sorely tested as a result of the statewide referendum limiting property-tax rates.

In other states most county libraries are governed by separate boards of trustees generally appointed by the governing body of the county. These boards for the most part enjoy the same powers and duties as those of municipal libraries. In fact some states, such as Colorado, Kentucky, and North Dakota, have a single law that applies to municipal and county libraries.

The city-county form of library organization, in which the principal city—usually the county seat—serves as the headquarters of the county library, has certain advantages. It provides unified library service for the county, allowing the book resources of the central library to be more widely distributed. The outlying agencies have their administration attached to the central library and are served and supervised by its staff. Oklahoma has a comparatively recent city–county library act, the purpose of which is:

> to foster and promote the establishment, maintenance and operation of city–county library systems in order to give all of the citizens of the counties affected hereby equal access to comprehensive library collections. It is the policy of the state to encourage the formation of such co-operative library systems to the end of avoiding unnecessary duplication in the maintenance and operation of public libraries and to stimulate the use of books and other library materials.[17]

This law applies to any county having within its boundaries a city of not less than a hundred thousand. It also provides for the creation of a city–county library commission consisting of eleven members, six to be appointed by the mayor of the city (subject to the approval of the governing body) and three by the county board of commissioners. The mayor and the chair of the county board are also ex officio members of the commission, entitled to vote on all matters. The board is authorized to levy a tax to provide its share of the funds necessary to establish and maintain city–county libraries.

The Systems Concept

Though some modest gains had been achieved in furthering public library development up to World War II through the instrumentality of county libraries, serious deficiencies in service continued to plague the public-library world. Carleton B. Joeckel in his monumental *National Plan for Public Library Service,* written with Amy Winslow and Lowell Martin, made the following assessment in 1948:

> Taken as a whole, library service in the United States falls far below the standards set by the best libraries—for three major reasons: First, one fourth of the American people live in places in which there are *no* libraries. Second, there are far too many administrative units: the typical unit is too small and too weak in economic ability to provide effective library service. And third, the average level of library support is so low that service in a large proportion of American libraries can be no better than mediocre.[18]

The plan that Joeckel and his associates drafted was designed to correct these weaknesses. Its broad principles have stimulated new ideas and new thinking about the future of public-library development in this country. More than any other influence, this plan has been responsible for introducing the "cooperative library system" concept as a dynamic force in public-library organization. Appearing at the same time as the *National Plan* was the general report of the Public Library Inquiry. Sponsored by the American Library Association, conducted by the Social Science Research Council under a grant from the Carnegie Corporation, and directed by Robert D. Leigh, this large-scale study examined the public library as a social institution. In the general report, *The Public Library in the United States,* Leigh confirmed and adopted the principal findings and recommendations of the *National Plan.*

Accepting the recommendations in these two reports, the

American Library Association in an official pronouncement declared:

> By developing plans for joint and cooperative programs, public libraries will be tied together in a network that goes far to equalize library opportunity and to bring the resources of the strongest libraries to all the people. Each separate taxing district in the country cannot maintain full library resources. Large cities and counties should be able to do so, providing in one or more centers facilities that meet full standards even though these are not achieved in all neighborhood units. Groups of smaller taxing districts can also provide access to resources that meet these standards, if they operate together in library systems. The immediate availability of the full range of facilities will differ from locality to locality, depending on population and wealth, but there is no reason for sub-standard facilities in any part of the country or in any section of a state.[19]

Thus the library-system concept came into existence. It is without a doubt one of the most significant ideas in the field of library government and holds great promise for achieving improved library services on a more adequate basis for every American.

(A word concerning terminology: an organization that provides cooperative library services is referred to interchangeably as a network, consortium, federation, authority, or agency. The most common term, however, is "library system," and the discussion that follows will generally use this expression for the sake of convenience.)

To determine the legal structure of an organization, one must examine the underlying documentation that authorizes its establishment. In general there are three instruments that provide the legal mechanism for establishing a library system: 1/ a statute enacted by a legislative body, 2/ articles of incorporation together with bylaws of the corporation, and 3/ a contract or a series of interlocking contracts. Although the library-system concept is in continuing development, a pattern of identifiable characteristics has emerged. It is possible to identify at least six governing elements.

First, library service under the system concept is usually based on a plan in which local libraries voluntarily cooperate with the state library agency to organize a network of systems. This network provides the resources needed to serve the population of the entire state. In the past there was little or no joint planning of any consequence: each library worked out its own salvation. The system concept, however, emphasizes statewide cooperation, with all types and sizes of libraries working together to achieve common goals. It is believed today that the quality of library service should not depend on where a person lives or on the wealth that a particular community happens to enjoy. Without this joint action and planning most American public libraries will never be able to meet the needs of all of their users.

Second, library systems must be large enough so that financial resources are sufficient to provide an adequate collection of lending and reference materials and services to satisfy the demands of users. But how large is large enough? Fortunately there are some usable guides that help provide an answer. A library system that coincides with the boundaries of a standard metropolitan statistical area, for example, is certainly of an adequate size. Another rule of thumb is to have the library system be counterminous with a natural trading area.

Third, the state helps fund the organization and operation of library systems with an aid program administered under rules and regulations prescribed by the state library agency. This aid is based on the rationale that public education is a function of state government, and since public libraries are part of the educational system of the state, those that are organized in systems are entitled to financial assistance. Although federal funds should also be made available for the promotion of library systems, state aid is the most crucial element. Cooperation is an old principle in the library world, but it has too often been a matter of lip service. With state aid serving as a catalytic agent, however, library cooperation really can be achieved.

Fourth, the system concept superimposes another government level over the many small independent libraries, organizing them into large units so as to extend and improve service over a wide area. State legislation creates a separate legal entity, the library-system board, thus conveying to the system the attributes of a municipal corporation. This is a brilliant device, since it does not interfere with the vested prerogatives of the existing library boards, which are usually loath to surrender their powers. The local libraries continue to enjoy their autonomy without diminution of authority, since the powers of the system board relate only to the activities and programs that the system itself operates. The system functions for most purposes as a "library's library," concerned primarily with serving the needs of its members.

Fifth, the system concept builds on existing strength in library resources and personnel and affords its members wide latitude in the type of programs they can pursue. The system board can decide, for example, to strengthen the library with the largest book collection so that it will function as the central library, and perhaps as the reference center, for the system. The board can also use a certain amount of the system's budget for improving the book collections of each member library. In short, the system is free to carry on a wide variety of activities.

Sixth, the final element in the system concept is the use of a library card that is honored by every library within the system. Patrons have full access to all books and services. In time this principle may be extended so that a statewide library card will be possible.

The system concept is predicated on the notion that library service is an indivisible whole, and that the distinctions between public, academic, school, and special libraries are essentially unimportant from the standpoint of the user. However, to this point most compacts are limited to one type of library, usually public or academic. New York has led the way in cutting across type-of-library boundaries in its Reference and Research Resources systems, which will be examined shortly. In most states the next step is to develop multitype systems, reflecting the essential unity of knowledge resources and the practice of some patrons of using public, school, academic, and other libraries interchangeably.

Public-Library Systems

Let us now examine how these elements are translated into law. New York was the first state to adopt the library-system concept on a statewide basis. In 1950 a law was approved providing for the establishment of "consolidated" and "federated" systems that were to be based on contractual agreements between participating libraries. But this law was superseded by the act of 1958 establishing "cooperative" library systems. Under the 1958 act the term "library system" is defined as follows: 1/ a library established by one or more libraries; 2/ a group of libraries serving an area including one or more counties in whole or in part; 3/ a library of a city containing one or more counties. In addition, a library system under the law must serve at least two hundred thousand persons or four thousand square miles of territory. Provisional approval, however, may be granted to a library system serving fifty thousand persons, provided that the area includes three or more political subdivisions. In such a case it is necessary to submit, for approval by the commissioner of education, a statisfactory plan of expansion of service to be followed during the ensuing five years.

The board of trustees of a proposed library system also must submit a plan of service, supported by such information as may be required by the commissioner. No plan can be approved unless it provides for a scheme of reciprocal borrowing whereby the participating libraries permit the loan of materials among each other on the same basis permitted by the library that owns the materials.

The commissioner is required to set the standards of service with which the library system must comply. The regulations relate to such matters as the book collection and the annual additions to the collection, circulation, maintenance of catalogs, number and locations of libraries and branches, hours open to the public, and number and qualifications of persons required to render adequate service. The regulations may establish standards that differ on the basis of total population, density of population, actual valuation of the taxable property within the area served, amount raised by taxation, or on such other basis as the commissioner finds necessary to provide for the equitable distribution of state aid.

Under the law the commissioner can revoke approval of a plan of service if the system fails to conform to its provisions. The system will therefore no longer be entitled to state aid until its plan is again approved. The law also provides that if the total sum raised by local taxation for the support of the library system and participating libraries is less than ninety-five percent of the average of the amounts raised for the same purpose for the two preceding calendar years, the state aid to which such system would otherwise be entitled would be reduced by twenty-five percent.

The law provides for state aid to the public-library systems in New York. Fixed annual grants are made to each system depending on whether it serves an entire county, a portion of a county, or more than one county. A fixed per capita grant is made to each system that submits an approved plan for the further development of the central library. An additional grant is made to a library system for the purchase of materials for the central library, as defined in regulations issued by the commissioner. Incidentally, ownership of such materials is vested in the system and not in the central library. Each system also receives a fixed per capita amount based on the population of the area served. In addition, there is a fixed amount per square mile of the area, depending on whether the system serves one or more than one county. Tied to state aid for systems ia a program designated as *local sponsor incentive aid*. Here, the funds are disbursed in accordance with a plan determined by the system board of trustees and paid to the member libraries. In effect this program constitutes direct state aid to all public libraries that are members of systems.

The total amount appropriated for state aid to library systems of all types in New York is in excess of $35 million per year, which is approximately $2 per capita. The formula for the distribution of aid as described above appears to be complex, but it is well founded. It attempts to promote larger government units of library service. It builds on existing strength by developing the resources of the central library. It endeavors to improve rural library service through its per-square-mile area grants. Finally, through the local sponsor incentive aid program, it seeks to strengthen each individual member library.

Pennsylvania was another of the pioneer states in the field of public-library systems. The Pennsylvania plan adopted in 1961 differs considerably from that of New York, but its overall objectives are the same. Essentially a state-aid scheme designed to improve all local libraries meeting standards prescribed in the act, the law does contain some, if not all, of the essential features of the system concept.

The Pennsylvania law authorizes the state librarian to designate up to thirty libraries throughout the state as district-library centers. This can include any public, state-college, Pennsylvania State University, or college or university library that agrees to serve as a district-library center. These centers are given the power to contract with the board of directors of any public library that desires to become a member. The latter are authorized to provide direct library service to persons residing within the district, to provide supplementary services to all local libraries within the district, and to exchange services with other centers. District-library centers receive a fixed per capita grant for each person residing in the district, paid by the state.

The state librarian designates four regional library resource centers to be located at the Free Library of Philadelphia, Pennsylvania State Library, Pennsylvania State University Library, and the Carnegie Library of Pittsburgh. Regional centers must make their research collections available to all state residents under rules and regulations determined by a board consisting of the head librarians of the four major institutions, with the state librarian acting as chair. Each center is eligible to receive from the state an amount not to exceed $100,000.

The Massachusetts and Rhode Island laws relating to library systems are quite similar. They both provide for the establishment, subject to approval by the state library agency, of five regional systems covering the entire state. The laws further provide that within each system one of the principal libraries is to be designated as a regional resource center. The center coordinates the development of resources within the system and furnishes supplementary services to member libraries and their patrons. The library agency can contract with the major public library in each state (Boston and Providence) to serve as statewide bibliographic backstops or "libraries of last recourse" to supply specialized reference and research materials. Regional resource centers are compensated by the state on a per capita basis of population. Boston and Providence receive additional funding from the state for their responsibilities as "libraries of last recourse."

The Illinois Library System Act of 1965 was modeled after the New York act of 1958. However, it made one significant contribution to the system concept: it was the first law to describe and delineate the legal powers of the system board. In fact it provides specifically that the system board is an independent corporate entity, a body politic with the right to hold title to property, to enter into contracts, to sue and be sued, and to take any action authorized by law.

California revised its public-library-systems act in 1977. The legislative declaration contained in the act telescopes the problems confronting public libraries today so cogently that it is reproduced below in its entirety:

> The Legislature finds and declares that it is in the interest of the people of the state to insure that all people have free and convenient access to all library resources and services that may enrich their lives, regardless of where they live or of the tax base of their local government. This finding is based on the recognition that:
>
> (a) the public library is a primary source of information, recreation and education to persons of all ages, any location or any economic circumstance.
> (b) The expansion of knowledge and the increasing complexity of our society create needs for materials and information which go beyond the ability of any one library to provide.
> (c) The public libraries of California are supported primarily by local taxes. The ability of local governments to provide adequate service is dependent on the taxable wealth of each local jurisdiction and varies widely throughout the state.
> (d) Public libraries are unable to bear the greater costs of meeting the exceptional needs of many residents, including the handicapped, non-English and limited English-speaking persons, those who are confined to home or in an institution, and those who are economically disadvantaged.
> (e) The effective sharing of resources and services among the libraries of California requires an ongoing commitment by the state to compensate libraries for services beyond their clientele.
> (f) The sharing of services and resources is most efficient when

> a common data base is available to provide information on where materials can be found.[20]

The *library federation*, a form of organization closely related to the library system, is to be found in a number of states, but is most common in Montana. The law defines a federation as a combination of libraries serving a multicounty, multicity, or city–county area, as designated by the state library commission. Two or more cities, towns, or counties can agree by contract to form a library federation by action of their respective boards of library trustees. The state library commission designates one of the parties to the agreement as the headquarters library for the federation area. The contract specifies the autonomy that the participating libraries may retain and apportions the expenses of the federation among them. The treasurer of one of the participating libraries has custody of the federation funds. The library federation's board of trustees has advisory powers only. Each participating library designates one of its board members to serve on the advisory board. Finally, the contract provides for participants to withdraw from the federation. It is of interest to note that in 1980 the Montana Library Commission for the first time distributed state aid to library federations from the proceeds derived from a state severance tax on coal.

Multitype Library Cooperation

Hardly had the public-library system idea been conceived when it became apparent that self-sufficiency could not be attained by any single library, whether it be public, academic, school, or special. The impossibility of such a goal became more evident as a result of the technological revolution and the information explosion that the post–World War II period was experiencing. Furthermore, it was also becoming clear that the existing forms of library organization, operating in isolation, were serving as barriers to the free flow and exchange of information and recorded knowledge. The new technology, coupled with the flood of print and nonprint materials required new patterns of library organization. The force of these movements helped to produce a new concept: multitype library cooperation.

As in the field of public-library systems, the state of New York was also one of the pioneers to grapple with multitype library cooperation. It inaugurated an interlibrary reference and research loan system that included most of the major public, academic, and special libraries in the state. The system became popularly known as the "3-R" system. For some years it operated without the sanction of any specific legislation, but state funds were appropriated to carry on this program.

In 1978 the system did receive official recognition by the passage of formal legislation. The act defined the term "reference and research library resources system" as "a duly chartered educational institution resulting from the association of a group of institutions of higher education, libraries, non-profit educational institutions, and other institutions organized to improve reference and research library resources service."[21] The service area of such a system must include no fewer than seven hundred and fifty thousand persons nor less than ten thousand square miles, comprise more than one county, and respect the integrity of the area of service of a public-library system.

Among the members of such a system must be at least four chartered degree-granting institutions of higher education of the four-year level whose libraries meet departmental standards. Additionally, there must be either: 1/ one such institution offering graduate programs for a master's degree whose library holds no fewer than two hundred and seventy-five thousand volumes and receives no fewer than three thousand periodical titles; or 2/ a public library that holds no fewer than four hundred thousand adult volumes and receives no fewer than fifteen hundred periodical titles. The member institutions of each system must be broadly representative of the chartered educational agencies, nonprofit organizations, and other special libraries providing services within the defined area of the system.

Each system must submit a plan of service to be approved by the commissioner of education. In approving, rejecting, or revoking plans of service or in promulgating regulations, the state library agency must consider the following:

1/ The prevention of unreasonable discrimination among the persons served by such library systems.
2/ The need for regional resources of sufficient size and varied in subject matter.
3/ The need for adequate books, materials (print and nonprint), and facilities for research and information.
4/ The need for outlets convenient in time and place for the sharing of library materials.
5/ The need for the economic and efficient use of public funds.
6/ The need for full use of local responsibility, initiative, and support of public-library service and the use of state aid in their stimulation but not as their substitute.[22]

Each reference and research library resources system, under the law, receives an annual grant from the state in excess of $125,000.

A number of states—Illinois, Texas, Wisconsin, and others—have provisions either in the state library act or the public-library-systems act designed to promote multitype library cooperation. The Illinois state library act, for example, lists as one of the powers of the state library the following:

> f. Promote and develop cooperative library networks operating regionally or statewide for providing effective coordination of the library resources of public, academic, school and special libraries, and to promote and develop information centers for improved supplemental library services for special library clientele served by each type of library or center.[23]

To facilitate the establishment of multitype library systems a public-authority mechanism has been suggested as a promising legal structure.[24] This relatively new device has been employed quite widely for the coordination of public mass transportation as well as for the delivery of other public services. A public authority is an independent unit of government created by the state to function side by side with existing duly constituted government entities. It has the ability to cross political boundaries, and, functioning as a separate level of government, it can be superimposed over many existing government bodies, particularly in a metropolitan area. Through the instrumentality of an interstate library compact, it can even cross state lines.

To create a library authority requires an act of the state legislature. Such an act must contain the following essential provisions: 1/ the geographical area of the authority must be specifically delimited; 2/ the purpose and powers of the authority must be fixed; 3/ the procedure for establishing the authority must be clearly defined; 4/ the governing body for directing the authority must be prescribed; and 5/ the method of funding the authority must be formulated. A model law for a metropolitan-area authority is presented in Appendix II.

The general purpose of the library authority would be to coordinate, facilitate, and improve access to the library resources of a given area so that they are made available to all residents. The authority would not be involved in the building of a separate library collection, for example, or in serving the public directly. These functions would continue to be performed by the libraries in the area. However, through a series of interlocking contracts with the public, academic, school, and special libraries, it would have the capacity to improve the overall services for the area. In effect the resources of the strongest library would be made available to the weakest.

With reference to the crucial matter of finance, the library authority should be supported primarily with funds administered through the state library agency. As the library authority would have the effect of equalizing library services for all the residents of the area, it is all the more reason why the state is the logical government body to support such a program. Of course, federal funds should also be made available to the authority. With these funds the authority, acting as a clearinghouse, would compensate those libraries that lend more materials than they borrow in a given calendar period, on a standard per-cost basis.

The authority form of organization is already on the statute books of Indiana for the establishment of public-library systems. It should be expanded to include academic, school, and special libraries.

An interesting example of a multitype library organization

based on the public-authority concept is the California Library Authority for Systems and Services, commonly referred to as CLASS. This organization was established, at the recommendation of the attorney-general of the state, under the California Joint Exercise of Powers Act. The act provides that two or more public agencies, if approved by their legislative or governing bodies, may exercise any power common to the contracting parties by entering into a joint-exercise-of-powers agreement. The parties to the joint agreement that constitute CLASS are the California State Library, University of California, California State University and Colleges, City of Los Angeles, County of Santa Clara, and Grossmont Community College. CLASS is governed by a Board of Directors made up of one representative from each of the member agencies, together with a nonvoting member representing private academic libraries and one representing special libraries. CLASS is a completely separate legal entity. Its debts, liabilities, or obligations do not constitute debts, liabilities, or obligations of any party to the agreement.

The purpose of the Authority is to assist the parties and other participating members in their efforts to create and implement a cooperative mechanism for library-program development and resource sharing, including but not limited to the following:

1/ to provide for the cooperative development and maintenance of common bibliographic and holdings data bases;
2/ to provide for development and implementation of an interlibrary-loan and delivery system;
3/ to provide for development and operation of systems for cooperative use of cataloging data, cooperative acquisitions, and other forms of resource sharing; and
4/ to provide for the development and implementation of library systems for information exchange.

Under the provisions of the joint agreement any library, public or private, including those of other states, may become a participating member of the Authority by executing an agreement with the Board of Directors in accordance with terms and conditions to be fixed in the bylaws adopted by the Board.

The joint agreement requires the Board to establish a Congress of Members, which must consist of representatives from each library participating in the Authority. The Congress adopts its own procedures for organizing, meeting, and voting, subject to the concurrence of the Board. One of the principal duties of the Congress is to elect representatives to an Authority Advisory Council made up of no more than twenty-one members. For purposes of electing representatives to the Council the participating libraries are grouped into seven segments: 1/ University of California Libraries; 2/ California State University and College Libraries; 3/ Community College Libraries; 4/ Public Libraries; 5/ State Library; 6/ Private Academic Libraries; 7/ Special Libraries. Representation on the Council is proportional, based on the average of the expenditures for library materials and binding, over the prior three years, of the total membership in each of the seven segments. The Advisory Council advises the Board of Directors on services, policies, procedures, fees, and other matters of concern to the membership. The presiding officer of the Council serves as a nonvoting member on the Board.

The chief executive officer of the Authority is appointed by the Board as well as the other members of the operating staff. The powers of the Board are set forth in detail in the joint agreement. Revenue for the Authority is derived from membership fees, grants, and payments for services rendered to the parties and participating agencies. The joint-exercise-of-powers agreement, signed by the six original parties, contains many other provisions, which taken together serve as the legal framework for the operations of the Authority. In addition to the joint agreement, CLASS is also governed by a set of bylaws.

Up to this point the discussion has been primarily concerned with cooperative library organizations whose legal structure is based on statutory law. Let us now examine a cooperative library organization whose legal basis is that of a nonprofit corporation. The best example is OCLC (Online Computer Library Center).

OCLC Inc. is a nonprofit corporation established under the laws of Ohio, with its principal office in Franklin County. Its articles of incorporation declare that the purpose of the organization is to maintain and operate a computerized library network and to provide processes and products for libraries and their users, including cataloging data. The corporation is managed by a Board of Trustees whose powers and duties are prescribed in the Code of Regulations, which has the same legal effect as bylaws. The corporation consists of three classes of members: General Members, Users Council Members and Trustee Members, with the voting powers of each class defined in the Code of Regulations.

In examining the Code of Regulations one finds that it contains a detailed description of the corporate structure of OCLC. The General Members of the corporation consist of public or private, academic or nonacademic libraries, and other entities that agree to comply with the contractual obligations of a participant in the corporation. General Members can vote only for delegates to the Users Council. Persons affiliated with General Members are eligible for appointment by the Board of Trustees and by the Users Council to serve on the respective committees thereof.

The Users Council is a unique governing arm of the corporation. Its purpose is to reflect and articulate the various interests of General Members and is empowered to elect six members of the Board of Trustees. The Users Council comprises those entities that contract with OCLC Inc. and provide under contract at least one percent of the computer terminals in the OCLC system. The number of votes to which a Users Council Member is entitled is determined by an intricate formula that is based on the number of terminals employed by the libraries that are affiliated with the Member. The Users Council is authorized to hold annual, regular, and special meetings as determined by the Council. The delegates to the Council are elected by General Members affiliated with a particular Users Council Member. The costs and expenses of the Council and the delegates are borne by the corporation.

The Board of Trustees of the corporation consists of fifteen members. Eight are elected by Trustee Members, three of whom must be connected with the library profession, with the remaining five selected from a variety of disciplines and community interests. Six members of the Board are elected by the Users Council. No more than two of these may be administrative or other professional employees of a Users Council Member. The president of the corporation is a member of the Board by virtue of office. The Founder Trustee of the corporation is also a member of the Board.

The OCLC pattern of organization has proven to be successful in developing a public utility that currently serves over twenty-two hundred libraries in all of the states and in Canada, with approximately three thousand terminals linked to OCLC computer facilities. It should also be observed that the decision made by OCLC that its services are to be made available primarily through regional and state library networks has helped to facilitate and strengthen multitype library cooperative activities and relationships throughout the country.

The ultimate aim of multitype library cooperation is a national network, the legal framework of which has not as yet been determined. However, it is not too early to give serious consideration to this matter, for there exists a variety of choices. Many believe that the coordinating arm of a national library network should be a federal agency. This could be the Library of Congress, for example, but preferably only after it has been formally designated the National Library of the United States. It could also be lodged in one of the divisions of the Department of Education, or it could be an independent federal library agency, such as the National Commission on Libraries and Information Science with increased powers. Another possible choice is a quasifederal entity, organized along the lines of the Federal Reserve System, that would strengthen the libraries of this nation, just as the Federal Reserve lends support to the banking community. Finally, there is a third choice, that of a nonprofit corporation chartered by the Congress, whose members would be state and regional library networks.

A federal coordinating agency would be responsible for allocating federal funds to state and regional library networks. It would also designate a group of libraries to serve as libraries of last resort in providing highly specialized materials on a nationwide basis. Specific libraries would be assigned areas of specialization for developing collections. The agency would also be responsible for facilitating international library-loan transactions as well as promoting other international library activities.

The *American Library Directory* lists three hundred and fifty-four organizations in forty-six states and the District of Columbia that are actively engaged in multitype library cooperation. Surely the time is ripe to harness these forces and mold a national library network to serve the people of this nation effectively.

VI SCHOOL LIBRARIES AND THE LAW

BECAUSE school libraries are so closely intertwined with instructional programs, it will be helpful to examine briefly the legal basis for public-school education in general. Public schools derive their legal authority from general provisions in state constitutions and from more detailed statutory enactments compiled in state codes on education. Article X, Section I, of the Illinois constitution is a typical example:

> A fundamental goal of the People of the State is the educational development of all persons to the limits of their capacity.
> The State shall provide for an efficient system of high quality public educational institutions and services. Education in public schools through the secondary level shall be free. There may be other free education as the General Assembly provides by law.
> The State has the primary responsibility for financing the system of public education.

The state codes on education are compilations of all of the permanent laws currently in force dealing principally with how the public schools are to be governed, administered, and financed. They also afford the legal basis for the instructional program, the provisions of which affect school libraries.

Legal Foundation of School Libraries

The legal authorization for the creation of school libraries followed closely on the heels of the formation of the free public school. New York in 1835 enacted a law permitting school districts to levy a tax of $20 to establish a library and a tax of $10 for each succeeding year, if approved by the voters. Two years later the General Court of Massachusetts passed a similar law. In 1848 Wisconsin in its first state constitution inserted a provision that earmarked the proceeds from the sale of public lands to be deposited in a "school fund," the interest of which was to be employed for support and maintenance of common schools and for the purchase of suitable libraries. The 1870 constitution of Virginia also had a provision requiring the furnishing of school libraries. By 1876 nineteen states and three territories had statutes permitting school districts to establish libraries and to levy taxes for their support.

Today every state has a law, express or implied, permitting the establishment of school libraries. The California law is the most comprehensive in this area. It virtually mandates that every school district provide school-library services for pupils and teachers, and further that the state Board of Education must adopt standards, rules, and regulations for these services. Libraries must be open for the use of pupils and teachers during the school day. In addition, they may be open at such other hours as the governing board determines. When open during evenings and Saturdays, the libraries must be under the supervision of certificated personnel—who cannot, however, be *required* to work such hours and also must be compensated in amounts determined by the governing board of the district as indicated on the salary schedule.

The law sets forth the powers of the school board with reference to the school library. It has the power to appoint the librarian and the staff, but they must qualify as librarians pursuant to state law. The board has also the power to make necessary rules and regulations not provided by the state Board of Education or the state Superintendent of Public Instruction, and not inconsistent therewith. It is also endowed with the power to exclude from school and school libraries all books and other publications of a "sectarian, partisan or denominational character." (The word "partisan," needless to say, is subject to considerable ambiguity.) Where no school library has been established, the board may contract with a county library or city library to furnish library services to the district. The law also allows the superintendent of schools in any county that has no library to establish a county school-library service for such elementary-school districts as may elect to participate. It is quite clear from the detail in which the school-library law of California is drafted that it is the intention of the legislature to ensure that every child in the state is provided with some form of school-library service.

There are a few miscellaneous provisions in the California law of further interest. The state Board of Education is expressly authorized to establish a consultant service to help districts establish and develop libraries in elementary and secondary schools. Another provision requires that no person may be employed as a school librarian without valid credentials. Finally, any librarian when employed full-time as a librarian, or partly as a librarian and partly as a teacher, has the rank of a teacher.

Laws of other states provide additional elements of school-library service. A number of state laws require that books for school libraries be selected from prescribed lists of titles approved or recommended by the state superintendent of public instruction or by a designated committee. The Nevada statute, for example, reads as follows:

> The superintendent of public instruction shall approve or disapprove lists of books for use in school libraries, but such lists shall not include books containing or including any story in prose or poetry the tendency of which would be to influence the minds of children in the formation of ideals not in harmony with truth and morality or the American way of life, or not in harmony with the Constitution and laws of the United States or of the State of Nevada.[25]

In Iowa the law merely provides that the state board of educational examiners must prepare annual lists of books suitable for use in school libraries and furnish copies to all county superintendents and board of education members. A recently enacted

Florida law on the subject of standards for book selection declares:

> (1) In the selection of textbooks, library books and other reading material used in the public school system, the standards used to determine the propriety of the material shall include:
> (a) the age of the children who normally could be expected to have access to the material.
> (b) The educational purpose to be served by the material.
> (c) The degree to which the material would be supplemented and explained by mature classroom instruction as part of a normal classroom instructional program.
> (d) No books or other material containing hardcore pornography or otherwise prohibited by s. 847.012 shall be used in the public school system of Florida.[26]

In Georgia and Nevada the minimum per-pupil amount expended for school libraries is fixed by statute at no less than $1. To ensure that school-library funds are not diverted to some other use the New York law authorizes the commissioner of education to withhold its share of public-school moneys from any city or district that uses these funds for any other purpose.

With reference to state aid for school libraries, a Massachusetts act adopted in 1977 authorizes the state Board of Education to provide for the establishment of school libraries and nonprint media services, including the acquisition or rental of materials and equipment, the employment of supplementary subprofessional personnel, and the use of consultative services. The funds to be appropriated for this purpose are to be disbursed to school districts on the basis of a formula that takes into consideration the following factors: the average expenditure over the immediately preceding five years for library resources, the current expenditure for such materials, the ratio of professional personnel to pupil enrollment, and the per-pupil expenditure for staff. The Board is also authorized to establish minimum standards for personnel, accessibility of resources, appropriations for library and nonprint media services, and local school-budget support. This law breaks new ground and should serve as a model for other states, since it authorizes the establishment of school libraries and media centers and provides that they are to be supported by a state-aid program separate from grants for general educational purposes.

In recent years there has been an attempt made to enact laws making school-library services mandatory. Bills have been introduced to achieve this purpose in a number of states, but failed to pass.

State and Local Regulations

In addition to statutory law, the departments of education and public instruction in the fifty states have rules and regulations that relate to school libraries and media centers. These are part of the administrative law of a state and have important implications for school librarians and media specialists.

Under the rules of the Illinois Board of Education, for example, every public school is required to provide a program of media services to meet its curricular and instructional needs. The rules also set forth the certification requirements for persons who are responsible for providing media services to students, teachers, and other school personnel. The standards for educational media programs, which are also incorporated into the rules and regulations issued by the Board of Education, were drafted by a joint committee of the state's Association of School Librarians, Audiovisual Association, and office of the superintendent of public instruction. They cover personnel, space requirements, selection of materials, type and quantity of materials, coordination of materials with the instructional program, and audiovisual equipment.

At the school-district level the rules and regulations of a board of education may also contain provisions that relates to the school library or media center, all of which have the force of law. Finally, an agreement between a board of education and a teachers' union will undoubtedly have provisions involving school-library personnel that are legally enforceable. The agreement between the Board of Education of the City of Chicago and the Chicago Teachers' Union, for example, has numerous provisions covering school libraries. Article 15—Librarians: Elementary and High School—is particularly illuminating and so is quoted here at length:

> 15-1. The standard (prescribed by the American Library Association in its *Standards for School Library Programs,* 1960, and supported by the Office of the Superintendent of Public Instruction in *Standards for School Library Programs in Illinois,* 1966) that there shall be one librarian for every 500 students or major fraction thereof shall be a goal toward which to work as funds become available.
> 15-2. The standards (prescribed by the American Library Association in its Standards for *School Library Programs,* 1960, and supported by the Office of the Superintendent of Public Instruction in *Standards for School Library Programs in Illinois,* 1966) that there shall be one library clerk for every 600 students or major fraction thereof shall be a goal toward which to work as funds can be made available.
> 15-3. The needs of the children shall be taken into consideration when determining the priority for assignment of additional library clerical help in high schools and elementary schools.
> 15-4. Adequate library facilities shall be provided in all new school buildings. In existing buildings, the BOARD shall provide such facilities as funds and space can be made available.
> 15-5. As a goal toward which the BOARD shall work as funds become available, provision shall be made for all primary school children in each elementary school to have one library period per week under the direction of the teacher-librarian.
> 15-6. In accordance with current policy, the number of children attending an upper grade center, middle school or elementary library class during one class period shall not exceed the number of tables, chairs, and/or other work areas available.
> 15-7. If the elementary school library facilities are to be used when the teacher-librarian is absent from the premises, guidelines for their use which are not in conflict with BOARD policy shall be established by the librarian, the principal, and the UNION's Professional Problems Committee of that school.
> 15-8. The program of the elementary teacher-librarian shall be so arranged as to provide for a minimum of four preparation periods per week for processing books and kindred library tasks, provided that, in addition, teacher-librarians shall be provided

not less than the average number of preparation periods accorded to other educational personnel in the school.
15-9. Every effort shall be made to send pertinent bulletins explaining library policies, practices, and procedures to the teacher-librarians.
15-10. One workshop or inservice meeting per school year for teacher-librarians shall be conducted at the area or district level during the regularly scheduled inservice time to provide information about new materials, equipment, techniques, and new approaches to library media service and the teaching of reading.
15-11. The principal shall designate a high school librarian to serve as department chairman, and such chairman shall attend all school department chairman meetings.
15-12. In accordance with current policy, the professional high school library staff in conjunction with the faculty and administration shall plan and implement a school-wide library program.
15-13. A librarian shall be included on all high school curriculum committees.
15-14. Clerical assistants in the schools shall not replace teacher-librarians in class instruction or library administration.
15-15. Where administratively possible, elementary librarians serving more than one school during one school week and high school librarians shall be assigned duties related only to the library programs.
15-16. On the day when a half-time librarian spends the morning at one building and the afternoon at another, he shall be assigned no duties outside of those resulting directly from his library assignment.
15-17. New buildings shall include adequate storage facilities for audiovisual equipment. In existing buildings, the BOARD shall provide the necessary storage facilities as funds and space can be made available.
15-18. To the extent that funds can be made available, the BOARD shall provide trained teacher aides to distribute and maintain audiovisual equipment in the elementary school library.
15-19. Trained audiovisual assistants shall be provided in the high school library as soon as funds can be made available.
15-20. A joint BOARD-UNION committee shall be continued in accordance with the provisions of Article 45-1 and 45-1.1 of this Agreement to review standards for elementary, middle, upper grade center and high school libraries, consider

professional problems other than grievances related to their operation, and present recommendations to the General Superintendent of Schools. This committee shall include at least two elementary, one middle school, one upper grade center and two high school librarians.

15-21. The BOARD agrees to furnish the UNION with a list of teacher-librarian vacancies to be published in the *Chicago Union Teacher* once a year.

It is clear from the details of these regulations that in this case both the Board of Education and the official teachers' organization recognize the importance of the school media center. Goals and standards of service are set, and provision made to prevent against intrusion on these standards.

Many states specify that school librarians and media specialists be considered as teachers. It follows from this that the laws, regulations, and other legal instruments that apply to teachers are *ipso facto* applicable to school librarians and media specialists as well.

Role of the Federal Government

Following the successful launching of Sputnik by the Russians, national officials became acutely aware of the deficiencies in our educational system. As a direct result Congress adopted the National Defense Education Act in 1958. The Act's declaration of policy pointed out that the national interest made it necessary for the federal government to assist in strengthening the educational establishment. The Act was to provide substantial assistance to the states and their local subdivisions in order to ensure trained personnel of sufficient quality and quantity to meet the defense needs of the United States. Thus a direct federal interest in education was asserted, based on the paramount national responsibility for defense, and this despite the fact that education is not discussed in the constitution.

The two most important provisions pertaining to school libraries were Titles III and XI of the Act. The purpose of Title III was to strengthen instruction at the elementary and secondary level in certain critical subjects. It made federal funds available for audiovisual and print materials, other than textbooks. The following excerpt from the *Guidelines* issued by the U.S. Office of Education to indicate a methodology for the selection of books is of interest:

Books and Other Printed and Published Materials

> Title III funds are to be used to strengthen instruction in science, mathematics, history, civics, geography, modern foreign languages, English, and reading. Therefore the requirements of the instructional program in these subjects should determine the choice of books and other printed materials. Book selection involves knowledge of the content and level of difficulty and an ability to judge the quality of the content as well as the format. Thus it is essential that the teachers who actually assign the materials to students take part in the selection of all books submitted on project applications. Good results can be achieved through acquisition projects when there is close cooperation between teachers and school librarians in acquiring the appropriate printed materials for present and planned courses in the critical subjects. All projects which include instructional materials should give evidence of teacher participation in their selection.

Title XI of the National Defense Education Act authorized the Commissioner of Education to arrange, through grants or contracts with institutions of higher education, for short-term or regular-session institutes for advanced study. This program, among other areas, included the use of the new media to improve the qualifications of individuals engaged as or preparing to become elementary- or secondary-school librarians. Each participant in such an institute was eligible to receive a stipend of $75 per week for the period of attendance together with an additional stipend of $15 per week for each dependent. In a single summer twenty-six colleges and universities throughout the country scheduled such institutes for school librarians at three levels of professional participation.

The significance of these school-library programs under this Act is that it placed school librarians in the same category with scientists, mathematicians, and other professionals who were critically needed to meet defense needs. Never before in the history of the United States had librarians been considered to be essential for the national defense.

The Elementary and Secondary Education Act (ESEA), adopted in 1965 during the era of the Great Society under Presidents Kennedy and Johnson, extended federal involvement. Title II of this Act provided grants for the acquisition of school-library resources, textbooks, and other instructional materials in public and private elementary and secondary schools. This program has been in continuous existence to the present day. In 1978, however, the Act was amended, with the transfer of the school-library program to Title IV-B. This Title provides funds for the acquisition of school-library resources, textbooks, and other print materials, and for the acquisition of instructional equipment in connection with the teaching of academic subjects.

The formula for the distribution of funds to each state under this Title is based on an allotment that bears the same ratio to the total amount appropriated for this purpose as the number of children aged five to seventeen inclusive bears to the number of children in all the states. To be eligible for a grant a state must submit a detailed plan that

1/ designates the state educational agency as the authorized body to administer the plan;
2/ sets forth a program under which the funds paid to a state will be expended for the programs and purposes stated in the act;
3/ provides assurances that the requirements relating to the participation of pupils and teachers in private schools will be met;
4/ describes the means by which a state educational agency will provide technical assistance to local educational agencies to enable them to participate fully in the program;
5/ provides assurances that the grants under this Title will be distributed to local school districts on an equitable basis;
6/ provides assurances that local school districts will not be required to submit applications for the program more than once every three years;

7/ provides assurances that the aggregate amount to be expended per student within the state from nonfederal sources for the program for the preceding fiscal year is not less than the amount per student expended for the second preceding fiscal year;
8/ sets forth the policies and procedures that give satisfactory assurance that federal funds made available will not be commingled with state funds;
9/ sets forth the means by which the state will make information and technical assistance available to private nonprofit-school officials who desire to make arrangements for children in those schools to participate in this program;
10/ sets forth a comprehensive plan for the coordination of federal and state funds for training activities;
11/ provides that a State Advisory Council be established.

The law also requires that the State Advisory Council be appointed by the state educational agency and be broadly representative of the cultural and educational resources of the state and of the public. It should comprise teachers, school administrators, school librarians, media specialists, guidance counselors, professionals with competence in special education for the physically and mentally handicapped, parents, students, and other interested members of the public. The function of the Council is to advise the state educational agency on policy matters involved in the preparation of the state plan and in its administration. It also is responsible for advising the agency in connection with the development of criteria for the distribution of funds and for the approval of applications for assistance under this Title.

Funds received under Title IV-B must be distributed by the state library agency to local school agencies according to the enrollments in public and private schools within a given district. However, higher per-pupil allocations may be made to 1/ school districts whose tax effort for education is substantially greater than that of the state, but whose per-pupil expenditure, excluding payments made under Title I of this Act, is no greater than that of the state; and 2/ school districts that have the greatest numbers or percentages of children whose education imposes a higher-than-average cost per child, such as children living in sparsely populated areas, and those from low-income families or families in which English is not the dominant language.

Local school districts are given complete discretion in dividing the funds they receive between the two basic purposes of Title IV-B: school-library resources and instructional equipment. The state educational agency, however, must ensure that each school district has adopted appropriate procedures for making that determination, including periodic consultation with teachers, librarians, media specialists, and other professional staff in the public and private schools.

The provision in the law that entitles children enrolled in private nonprofit elementary and secondary schools to participate in the benefits of the Title IV-B program is a major breakthrough. In the past the doctrine of separation of church and state has prevented schools affiliated with religious denominations from receiving public tax funds. To overcome this constitutional objection Title IV-B was drafted so that the financial assistance that it provides is directed toward the student and not the institution. The law merely authorizes local educational agencies to consult with private-school officials so that their students can receive the benefits of the Title IV-B program. The law is clear that the control of funds provided under the statute, and the Title to the library resources and instructional equipment, rests with the local educational agency. The provision of services pursuant to this phase of the program is provided by a public agency through a contract "with a person, an association, agency, or corporation who or which in the provision of such services is independent of such private school and of any religious organizations, and such employment of contract shall be under the control and supervision of such public agency, and the funds provided under this subchapter shall not be commingled with state or local funds." However, the library resources and instructional equipment that can be made available to private schools must be "secular, neutral and non-ideological."

If no program under Title IV-B is undertaken in a given school district, then the state educational agency must make the necessary contractual arrangements with a nonprofit private agency or organization under which the children in private schools will be able to participate in the services and materials provided under this Title. If a state is prohibited by law from providing the participation in such programs of children enrolled in private schools, then the Secretary of the U.S. Department of Education must arrange for the provision of services to such children. Finally, expenditures for programs to serve children in private schools must be equal to expenditures for programs for children in the public schools, consistent, of course, with the number of children to be served.

Let us now examine the rules and regulations issued by the U.S. Department of Education that are applicable to Title IV-B. Under the regulations the term "academic subjects" means, but is not limited to the arts, civics, economics, English, geography, history, the humanities, industrial arts, mathematics, foreign languages, reading, and science. "Instructional equipment" is that which is appropriate for use in teaching or learning academic subjects. The eligibility of instructional equipment is determined by its intended use: general-purpose classroom or library furniture, or physical-education equipment, is not considered "instructional"; musical equipment, if used for regular instructional purposes, is so considered.

The regulations provide that the state educational agency must develop a plan for monitoring projects approved under this Title in order to determine whether there has been satisfactory compliance with the provisions of the law. Within sixty days after a monitoring visit it must submit a written report to the local educational agency of its findings. If the local agency disagrees with the findings, it may make a reply in writing, to which the state agency must respond. All monitoring reports, replies, and responses are public documents and are available to the public for inspection.

State library agencies are also required under the regulations to develop standards for local educational agencies. The standards ensure that all equipment and materials acquired with federal funds are of adequate quality and quantity and are used solely for instructional purposes.

Finally, the regulations provide that if a local educational agency concentrates Title IV-B funds on a particular group, attendance area, grade, or age level, the local agency must ensure equitable participation by children enrolled in private schools who have the same needs, and are in that particular group, attendance area, grade, or age level. A local educational agency, however, may not use Title IV-B funds to finance the existing level of instruction in a private school or otherwise benefit the school.

In addition to the regulations issued by the U.S. Department of Education, there are also rules or guidelines that each state educational agency adopts in administering the funds provided under Title IV-B. Local school districts must abide by these rules to be eligible for grants under this program. For example, the Illinois Department of Public Instruction guidelines relating to Title IV-B cover 1/ state plan administration; 2/ development, revision, and application of standards; 3/ allocation and selection of materials; 4/ project proposals; 5/ conditions under which materials will be made available; and 6/ fiscal control and fund accounting.

The federal-assistance program as provided in ESEA for the benefit of children enrolled in nonpublic schools has been on the statute books for fifteen years, and the legality of its provisions has not been challenged as being in violation of the First Amendment "respecting an establishment of religion." In this connection, however, it should be noted that there have been three cases before the U.S. Supreme Court that involved the constitutionality of state laws that provided for the free lending of textbooks, instructional materials, and instructional equipment to children attending private elementary and secondary schools. The first case was Board of Education v. Allen (392 U.S. 236), decided in 1968. In this suit the plaintiffs sought to invalidate a New York law that required local school districts to lend textbooks free of charge to all students in grades seven to twelve, including those in private schools. The trial court held the law unconstitutional and entered a summary judgment for the plaintiffs. The judgment was appealed to the New York Court of Appeals, which reversed the ruling of the trial court. Thereupon the case moved to the U.S. Supreme Court. The highest court in the land ruled that the New York law did not violate the First Amendment of the Constitution, by a six-to-three decision, with Justice Douglas filing a strong, fourteen-page dissenting opinion. The majority opinion was based on the following rationale:

1. The express purpose of the statute was the furtherance of educational opportunities for the young, and the law merely makes available to all children the benefits of a general program to lend textbooks free of charge, and the financial benefit is to the parents and children, not to schools.
2. There is no evidence that religious books have been loaned, and it cannot be assumed that public school authorities are unable to distinguish between secular and religious books or that they will not honestly discharge their duties to approve only secular books.
3. Parochial schools in addition to their sectarian function, perform the task of secular education, and, on the basis of this meager record, the Court cannot agree with appellants that all teaching in a sectarian school is religious, or that the intertwining of secular and religious training is such that secular textbooks furnished to students are in fact instrumental in teaching religion.
4. In the absence of specific evidence, and based solely on judicial notice, it cannot be concluded that the statute results in unconstitutional involvement with religious instruction or violate the Establishment Clause.

The next case to come before the U.S. Supreme Court was Meek v. Pittenger (421 U.S. 349), adjudicated in 1975. This case involved a Pennsylvania statute that authorized the secretary of education directly or through the intervention of school districts to purchase textbooks and, upon individual request to lend them free of charge to all children in kindergarten through grade twelve attending a nonpublic school. The total amount that could be expended for textbooks was limited to $10 per pupil. It also authorized the secretary of education directly or through the intervention of school districts to purchase instructional materials and equipment and to lend them to nonpublic schools without any charge. The total amount that could be expended for this purpose was limited to $25 per pupil.

A number of individuals and organizations filed a complaint in the Federal District Court challenging the constitutionality of this act. The District Court upheld the validity of the textbook and instructional materials programs but invalidated the instructional-equipment program on the ground that it could be diverted to religious purposes. The case was appealed to the U.S. Supreme Court, which ruled that the provision relating to instructional materials was *also* unconstitutional. Justice Stewart delivered the opinion:

> The direct loan of instructional materials and equipment to non-public schools . . . has the unconstitutional primary effect of establishing religion because of the predominant religious character of the schools benefiting from the Act since 75% of Pennsylvania non-public schools . . . are church related or religiously affiliated. The massive aid that non-public schools thus receive is neither indirect nor incidental, and even though such aid is ostensibly limited to secular instructional material and equipment the inescapable result is the direct and substantial advancement of religious activity.

The most recent case is Wolman v. Walter (433 U.S. 229), heard in 1977. The facts in this case, insofar as they relate to textbooks, instructional materials, and instructional equipment, are quite similar to *Meek*, summarized above. Attorneys for the defendants argued that *Meek* involved a program of direct loans to nonpublic schools, whereas in the present case the loans were made to students and parents. The court rejected this argument and declared: "In our view, however, it would exalt form over substance, if this distinction were found to justify a result different from that in *Meek*." Consequently the court ruled that the loans of instructional materials and equipment violate the First Amendment.

These three decisions make it quite clear that public funds may be used to provide for the lending of textbooks to students enrolled in private schools, but not for the lending of instructional materials and equipment. As noted above, the provisions of Title IV-B of ESEA regarding assistance to children enrolled in private schools are quite similar to those that were involved in the three cases that have been analyzed. However, since there has been no direct legal challenge instituted against Title IV-B, its provisions will continue to remain in effect until it is challenged and the U.S. Supreme Court renders a decision.

Thus school libraries and school media centers, besides being indirectly affected by the range of law that relates to public and nonpublic schools, are also directly influenced by statutes, regulations, and court decisions specifically dealing with library matters. School librarians, no less than practitioners in other types of libraries, should be aware of the legal authorizations and strictures under which they function. Indifference to legal precepts is not justified on the grounds that these are matters for school authorities alone.

VII ACADEMIC LIBRARIES AND THE LAW

In order to understand the legal structure of academic libraries, one must first examine that of the universities and colleges they serve. From the standpoint of law, institutions of higher education fall into two classes—private and public.

Private academic institutions owe their legal existence either to a corporate charter or articles of incorporation. In an earlier period colleges and universities were granted charters by the states. In the absence of a provision reserving the state's right to alter, amend, or annul the charter, these institutions were free to carry on their educational activities with little or no interference. This principle was firmly established in the famous case of Dartmouth College v. Woodward (17 U.S. 517). In 1819 New Hampshire sought to convert Dartmouth College into a state university. The trustees of the college objected to this legislation and filed a suit to prevent its implementation. On appeal the case came before the U.S. Supreme Court, which held that the legislation was unconstituional. The court ruled that the charter granted by the British crown to the trustees of Dartmouth College in 1769 is a contract and that it was not dissolved by the Revolution. The state legislature could not alter it, for such a move would constitute a violation of Article I, Section X, of the U.S. Constitution, which forbids a state to pass laws impairing the obligation of contracts.

As a result of this decision state legislatures began to enact general laws, rather than special acts, authorizing the incorporation of private institutions of higher education, the legal authority for whose operation would be the articles of incorporation. Universities and colleges are designated as nonprofit corporations; as such, they enjoy perpetual succession and the right to exercise all powers needed to effect the purposes set forth in the articles of incorporation. Among these are the right to hold title to property, enter into contracts, accept gifts, sue and be sued, and enact bylaws that are enforceable at law providing they are consistent with the articles of incorporation. Furthermore, private academic institutions are generally exempt from income, property, and sales taxes, and gifts made to them are tax exempt, as well.

The legal basis for public universities and colleges is to be found in state constitutions, acts of state legislatures, and ordinances of municipal governments. Many constitutions have provisions relating to the state university. Sometimes they afford it a high degree of freedom. For example, in State v. University of Minnesota (236 Minn. 452), the Supreme Court of Minnesota held that the Board of Regents of the University of Minnesota is more than an "administrative agency." The court declared that it is a body corporate created by the state constitution and its charter may be amended only by action of the people of the state. Additionally, it held that the Board of Regents is endowed with the power to govern the university, free from interference by either the legislature or courts so long as it remains within its constitutional powers.

Where there is no constitutional provision, public universities and colleges owe their legal existence to acts of the legislature or ordinances of a municipal body. A statute authorizing the establishment of a public institution of higher education generally begins by describing its purpose. It then provides for its governance through the appointment of a board of trustees or regents. The powers of the board are explicitly set forth in detail; they include the power to adopt rules and regulations for the school's administration and operation. Although some public colleges and universities are granted the power to levy taxes, the funding for most of them is derived from appropriations voted by the legislature from the general revenues of the state or by appropriations from duly authorized municipal sources.

Regulations of Governing Boards

Examination of these charters, articles of incorporation, state constitutions, laws, and ordinances reveals hardly any mention of libraries. For this, one must consult the rules and regulations promulgated by the governing boards of universities and colleges. Here may be set forth the professional status of the library director, and such matters as tenure, academic rank, sabbatical leave, and retirement of library staff. The rules also generally provide for a library committee, council, or board made up of faculty members to assist the director in the allocation of book funds and the formulation of library policy. Since the rules and regulations have the sanction of law, it is essential that they include such provisions as those described above.

The following regulations of the University of Illinois exemplify the provisions usually made:

Article VI—The Campus Library

a) The Campus Library includes all books, pamphlets, serials, maps, music scores, photographs, prints, manuscripts, micro-reproductions, and other materials purchased or acquired in any manner and preserved and used by it to aid students and investigators. Such materials may include sound, electronic and magnetic recordings, motion picture films, slides, film strips, and other appropriate audio-visual aids.
b) The Campus Library shall be in the charge of the director of the library.
c) The director shall be responsible for the arrangement and care of the Campus Library and for the organization of its staff and shall make an annual report to the Chancellor on the condition and needs of the library and on the work of the staff.
d) With the approval of the Chancellor, the director may establish branches on the campus when in his opinion efficiency in reference work, circulation, cataloging, ordering and other matters of library administration, and the general welfare of the campus, college, school, department or other unit will thereby be promoted: and when such action has been

taken, the director may delegate appropriate powers to the assistants in charge of such branches. Appointments to the staff of branch libraries established under this subsection and the advancement of staff will be recommended with the advice of the executive officer of the unit(s) served by such library.

e) The director shall be appointed annually by the Board of Trustees on the recommendation of the Chancellor with the concurrence of the President of the University. On the occasion of each such appointment, the Chancellor shall have the advice of the Library Committee of the Senate.

f) Members of the Campus Library staff shall be appointed by the Board of Trustees on the recommendation of the director of the library, the Chancellor and the President and may be given appropriate academic rank.

g) The Standing Library Committees of the Senate shall advise the director regarding the apportionment of book funds and other matters pertaining to the Campus Library.[27]

In the area of multitype library cooperation, there is state legislation that affects academic libraries. New York, for example, requires the state university and New York City's Board of Higher Education to provide for the use by state residents of the libraries of institutions of higher education under their jurisdictions. The Illinois Library Systems Act designates the libraries of the University of Illinois and Southern Illinois University as statewide Research and Reference Centers. They receive annual grants from the state to strengthen their book collections. Similarly, the Pennsylvania State University Library has been designated by law as a Regional Library Resource Center in that state. The Pennsylvania law also provides for a system of District Library Centers in which the library of any state college or private college or university may agree to participate in this program in return for state-aid funds.

Collective bargaining for academic librarians has become a matter of considerable concern in recent years. One of the principal legal questions is that of the bargaining unit with which they should be affiliated. Should it be the unit that covers the faculty, or should librarians have their own bargaining unit, or perhaps be represented by a unit that includes all types of employees of a given institution? In general the National Labor Relations Board has ruled that librarians connected with institutions of higher education are professionals belonging in the same bargaining unit as members of the faculty.

Another important issue in recent years has been that of faculty tenure for academic librarians. The legal basis for tenure is derived from the power that is conferred, by statute or corporate charter, upon the governing boards of universities and colleges to make rules and regulations and promulgate bylaws for the administration of these institutions. In the case of some public institutions the legal authority for faculty tenure is actually spelled out in a statute. Section 36.15 of *Wisconsin Statutes Annotated*, for example, contain this provision:

> If in any institution all professional librarians with appropriate degrees as determined in accordance with that institution's policies, have formerly been ranked as faculty, all present and future appointments of professional librarians with appropriate graduate degrees in such institutions shall be as ranked faculty, except in those institutions where the chancellor and faculty designate that such appointments shall be as academic staff.

Some years ago a study of eighty colleges and universities, *Tenure in American Higher Education*,[28] reported the following breakdown: twenty-seven institutions had a tenure plan based on statutes or bylaws; twenty had a statement on tenure approved by the governing board; nine relied on a tenure plan contained in a document drafted by the administration, such as a faculty manual; in two institutions the tenure plan was set forth in a faculty constitution; five institutions indicated a formal definition of tenure but did not state the source; fourteen reported that although tenure was informally organized, it was not spelled out in a document; and three reported no formal or informal plan of tenure.

It is clear that governing boards, with their power to make rules and regulations and to draft bylaws, are able to extend tenure to professional librarians. In the absence of a statutory mandate, however, it is unlikely that they can be *compelled* to do so. Thus the issue of tenure is more a question of administrative practice and decision than one of law *per se*.

The report on *Faculty Tenure* issued in 1973 by the Commission on Academic Tenure in Higher Education makes the following recommendation:

> 37. The commission recommends that if nonteaching personnel are made eligible for academic tenure, the institution should develop for these groups [which includes professional librarians] tenure standards equivalent in rigor to those applicable to the teaching faculty.

Although there is a considerable body of case law involving institutions of higher education—primarily in the realm of tax exemptions, tort liabilities, exercise of corporate powers, perpetuation of trusts, academic tenure, and related matters—there are very few legal cases in which an academic library is directly involved. The only one of importance that this writer was able to discover is State *ex rel.* Little v. Regents of the University of Kansas (55 Kan. 389), adjudicated in 1895. It appears that the Board of Regents of the University of Kansas imposed an annual library fee of $5 on all students. A suit was brought by the Attorney General of the state challenging the legality of this measure. The Board of Regents contended that it could lawfully charge a fee for the use of the library under its power to make rules and regulations. The Supreme Court of Kansas, however, held that the library fee was illegal:

> If the regents may collect $5.00 for the use of the library, why may they not collect also for the use of the rooms of the building and of its furniture? Why may they not impose fees for walking in the campus, or for the payment of the instructors. . . . The library is provided for permanent use. Each volume, with proper care, may be used by a great number of students and for a long term of years. The library as a whole is subjected to wear and tear, but only in the same manner as furniture and other properties furnished by the state. The buildings, furniture, library and apparatus, as well as the services of the faculty, are furnished and paid for by the state. These, we hold, . . . are free to all residents of the state who are entitled to admission into the university. The regents have no power to raise a fund to be managed and disposed of at their discretion, by charging fees for

> the use of the library, or under any other claim for any other purpose, unless expressly authorized to do so by law.

Whether the opinion of this court can serve as a bar against the imposition of a fee for the use of an electronic data base in a library of a public institution of higher education remains yet to be determined definitively.

Federal Provisions

We turn now to examine federal legislation designed expressly to assist academic libraries. The most important piece of legislation in this area is Title II of the Higher Education Act. First passed in 1965, the Act was amended and revised extensively in 1980. Title II consists of four parts: Part A—College Library Resources; Part B—Library Training, Research and Development; Part C—Strengthening Research Library Resources; and Part D—National Periodical System.

Part A of Title II provides for a program of resource-development grants to be made available to institutions of higher education. The grants, which may not exceed $10,000, are made upon application by an institution subject to the following conditions: 1/ provision of information about the institution and its resources as prescribed in regulations by the Secretary of Education; 2/ satisfactory assurance that the applicant will expend for all library materials an amount not less than the average annual aggregate amount or the average amount it expended for such purposes per full-time equivalent student during the two fiscal years preceding the fiscal year for which assistance is sought; 3/ maintenance of fiscal controls, and funding procedures as necessary to ensure proper disbursement of and accounting for federal funds paid to the applicant; and 4/ provision of such reports as the Secretary may require. Grants under this part may be used only for library materials, including binding. Such funds may also be used for the establishment and maintenance of networks for sharing library resources with other institutions of higher education.

Part B of Title II provides for a program of grants in three areas: library training, library research, and library development. The grants for training may be employed for the following purposes: 1/ to assist in covering the cost of courses of training or study, including short-term or regular-session institutes; 2/ to establish and maintain fellowships or traineeships with stipends, including travel allowances and subsistence for fellows and others undergoing training and their dependents; and 3/ to establish, develop, or expand programs of library and information science, including new techniques of information transfer and communication technology. The law provides that at least fifty percent of the library-training grants must be made for fellowships and traineeships. In the area of library research, funds are available for research and demonstration projects related to improvement of libraries, training in librarianship, and information technology. Finally, in the area of library development, there are grants available for a variety of special purposes, particularly in the field of cooperation and joint use of facilities.

Part C of Title II provides for a program of grants designed to strengthen research-library resources. These funds are available only to institutions with "major research libraries." The law defines a major research library as a public or private nonprofit institution of higher education, an independent research library, or a state or other public library having a library collection that is available to qualified users and meets the following requirements:

a) makes a significant contribution to higher education and research;
b) is broadly based and is recognized as having national or international significance for scholarly research;
c) is of a unique nature, and contains material not widely available; and
d) is in substantial demand by researchers and scholars not connected with that institution.

In disbursing grants under this part the Secretary is required to make a broad and equitable geographical distribution throughout the nation.

Part D of Title II deals with a national periodical system. It must first assess the feasibility and advisability of such a system and then—if its findings are positive—prepare a design for a system that can provide access to a comprehensive collection of periodical literature to public and private libraries throughout the United States. To accomplish this the law authorizes the establishment of a nonprofit National Periodical System Corporation, which is not to be considered an agency or establishment of the U.S. government. The law further provides that any design for a national periodical system must:

1/ acquire current and past issues of periodicals and preserve and maintain a dedicated collection of such documents;
2/ provide information on periodicals to which the system can ensure access, including those circulated from private-sector sources, and cooperate in efforts to improve bibliographic and physical access to periodicals;
3/ make such periodicals available through libraries, by loan, photoreproduction, and other means;
4/ cooperate with and participate in international borrowing and lending activities as may be appropriate for such purposes;
5/ ensure that copyright owners who do not wish to participate in such system are not required to participate;
6/ ensure that copyright fees are fixed by the copyright owners for any reproduction or dissemination of a document delivered through the system;
7/ complement and not duplicate activities in the private sector to provide access to periodical literature;
8/ ensure, to the maximum extent feasible, that such system not adversely affect the publication and distribution of current periodicals, particularly scholarly periodicals of small circulation; and
9/ ensure coordination with existing programs to distribute periodical literature, including programs of regional libraries and programs involving interlibrary-loan networks.

The law also provides that the design must make provisions for the role, if any, of the Corporation in the governance, administration, and operation of the system. In addition, the design must indicate an estimate of the cost involved in setting up such a system.

The Corporation is to be governed by a Board of Directors consisting of fifteen members, fourteen to be appointed by the President with the advice and consent of the Senate, plus the operating director of the Corporation. The members of the Board may not receive compensation, nor are they deemed to be employees of the federal government. The Corporation, however, is authorized to use the U.S. mails in the same manner and under the same conditions as departments and agencies of the government. The proposed design cannot be implemented until it is approved by a joint resolution of Congress.

The import of the National Periodical Center goes beyond periodicals as such. It constitutes a federally authorized corporation meant explicitly to serve libraries across the country, a further step in the federal interest in coordinating access to resources for study and research. Questions other than legal issues have so far held up implementation of the proposal.

Another important federal act directly affecting academic institutions with medical libraries is the Medical Library Assistance Act, adopted in 1965 and amended several times since. The purpose of this law is: 1/ to assist in the training of medical librarians and other information specialists in the health sciences; 2/ to assist in the compilation of data that will facilitate the distribution and utilization of knowledge and information relating to scientific, social, and cultural advancements in sciences related to health; 3/ to assist in the conduct of research in the field of medical library science, and in the development of new techniques, systems, and equipment for processing, storing, retrieving, and distributing information in the health sciences; 4/ to assist in establishing, expanding, and improving the basic resources of medical libraries and related facilities; 5/ to assist in the development of a national system of regional medical libraries, each of which would have facilities of sufficient depth and scope to supplement the services of other medical libraries within the region served by it; and 6/ to provide financial support to biomedical scientific publications.

The law designates the Board of Regents of the National Library of Medicine to serve as the National Medical Library Assistance Advisory Board. The function of the Board is to advise the Secretary of the U.S. Department of Health and Human Services in preparing general regulations and setting policy.

The Secretary is authorized to make grants for each of the purposes listed above, including the key provision for a national system of regional medical libraries. Grants for establishing such units may be used for the following purposes: 1/ acquisition of books, journals, and other similar materials; 2/ cataloging, binding, and other procedures for processing library materials; 3/ acquisition of duplicating equipment to facilitate the use of the resources of the library; and 4/ acquisition of equipment for the speedy transmission of materials from the regional centers to local libraries. Grants may be made only to medical libraries that agree to increase their resources so as to be able to provide adequate supportive services to all libraries in the region. In awarding grants the Secretary must give priority to those collections having the greatest potential of fulfilling the needs for regional medical libraries. Grants for basic resource materials may exceed fifty percent of the library's annual operating expenditures. Unlike the periodical program, the regional-medical-library program is in place and involves a continuing federal legal commitment to academic- and research-library resources.

Another federal law of concern to academic libraries is the Higher Education Facilities Act, adopted in 1963 but suspended during the Nixon era. In signing this measure President Johnson declared that "this new law is the most significant education bill passed by Congress in the history of the Republic." (It is interesting to observe that the Higher Education Facilities Act was passed almost a hundred years after the Morrill Act of 1862, popularly referred to as the Land Grant Act.

The Higher Education Facilities Act provided for a five-year program of grants to institutions of higher education for the purpose of constructing and rehabilitating academic facilities required to accommodate the student explosion of that day. The Act defined academic facilities to include library buildings. For fiscal year 1966 Congress authorized an appropriation of $460 million for this purpose, and it is significant to note that one-third of the funds appropriated for fiscal year 1965 was absorbed in funding library-building projects.

VIII FEDERAL LIBRARY LEGISLATION

THE federal government was a latecomer to the field of library legislation. During its first hundred years the government took hardly any notice of libraries other than those that served the federal establishment. This apparent neglect is understandable in light of the nature of the U.S. government system. Ours is a government of dual sovereignty; Congress has only the powers that are expressly delegated to it in the U.S. Constitution. Furthermore, under the Tenth Amendment to the Constitution, the powers not expressly delegated to the Congress nor prohibited to the states are reserved to the states or to the people. Since the Constitution mentions neither education nor libraries, the federal government at first paid little or no attention to them.

The earliest serious recognition of libraries by the national government was indicated by a report issued in 1876 by the Bureau of Education. *Public Libraries in the United States of America: Their History, Condition and Management* appeared in two parts. Part I was a voluminous work of over eleven hundred pages offering useful library statistics from across the country, together with numerous articles on every branch of library economy. Part II of the report consisted of *Cutter's Rules for a Printed Catalog*.

Increased Federal Participation

Subsequent to the publication of the 1876 report, Congress, over a period of years, enacted a number of laws of considerable importance to libraries. Among these were the establishment of a depository-library system for the free distribution of public documents, provisions for the importation of books by libraries free of duties of any kind, reduced postal rates for printed library materials, the sale of catalog cards by the Library of Congress, and the free distribution of books for the blind to libraries.

As the library movement in America expanded, there arose a demand for a federal library agency. Although its purpose was not clearly delineated, it was generally agreed that such a body would be beneficial for the coordination of library service on a national scale. After years of vigorous campaigning by the American Library Association, a permanent Library Services Division was finally established in the U.S. Office of Education in 1938. In the words of John W. Studebaker, Commissioner of Education at the time, the function of the Division was "to gather facts and to undertake practical research in the field of librarianship." Having gained a foothold in the national establishment, librarians began to strive for federal aid in earnest. This move was spurred on by the greater efforts that were being made on behalf of education to obtain federal assistance for schools. For the library world the first fruits of victory came in 1956, with the passage of the Library Services Act during the Eisenhower administration. This measure, intended primarily as a demonstration program, provided a meager program of federal funds for public libraries serving rural communities of under ten thousand inhabitants.

In 1963 a major breakthrough at the federal level promised to have far-reaching implications. It began with a message to Congress on education delivered by President Kennedy. In his opening remarks he declared:

> . . . for the individual, the doors to the schoolhouse, to the library and to the college lead to the treasures of our open society; to the power of knowledge—to the training and skills necessary for productive employment—to the wisdom, ideals and culture which enrich life—and to the creative, self-disciplined understanding of society needed for good citizenship in today's changing and challenging world.

In the course of his recommendations Kennedy referred directly to libraries no fewer than six times and outlined three specific programs for strengthening and improving public, college, and university facilities. This was the first time that the presidential spotlight had been focused on library problems with such clarity and intensity.

There followed in rapid succession a series of enactments that ultimately covered all types of libraries: public, school, academic, and special. The amount and extent of federal library legislation approved in 1964 and 1965 was indeed impressive. It included the Library Services and Construction Act, Elementary and Secondary Education Act, Higher Education Act, and Medical Library Assistance Act. All of these laws remain on the statute books.

Library Services and Construction Act

Previous chapters have described the salient provisions of these acts, with one exception. The Library Services and Construction Act (LSCA) was adopted in 1964 and amended on several occasions. At this writing it consists of four titles: Title I—Services; Title II—Construction; Title III—Interlibrary Cooperation; Title IV—Older Readers Services.

From its inception LSCA provided grants to state library agencies for the purpose of extending public-library services to areas where they were inadequate or nonexistent. This law grants a fixed minimum allotment to each state. Any sums remaining after the minimum allotments have been made are distributed on the basis of population. However, a built-in factor is provided that takes into account the per capita income of each state. Every state library agency is required to submit a basic plan setting forth the programs and projects for which the funds are to be used, and in addition is required to submit a separate annual program for all four titles. Each agency, within the rules and regulations set forth by the Secretary of Education, determines how the funds are to be used and is responsible for channeling them to local public libraries.

A number of additions have been tacked on to Title I. Among these are provisions for making public-library services more accessible to persons who are physically handicapped, institutionalized, or otherwise disadvantaged; for improving and strengthening state library agencies; and for strengthening major urban resource libraries. The latter provision was adopted in 1977 at the behest of the Urban Libraries Council.

The annual appropriations voted for LSCA have fluctuated. The peak was fiscal year 1967, under President Johnson, when more than $75 million was approved. During the Nixon administration not only were LSCA funds reduced, but a substantial portion was impounded by the President after being approved by Congress. These funds were released only after a court order had so decreed. Under the Carter administration federal funding for public libraries had reached the level of $67.5 million per year.

At this juncture it is important to point out that when President Kennedy made his significant proposal for federal assistance to libraries in 1963, the Library Services Act, which had been on the statute books since 1956, was not rewritten. It was merely amended and became Title I of LSCA. No substantive changes were introduced in Title I, either relating to the purpose of the Act or how the funds were to be employed. The only basic change was the removal of the word "rural" before the word "areas" so that it would be applicable to cities as well. In essence, Title I of LSCA continued to be a demonstration program, not a plan for federal sharing in the cost of long-established public libraries.

The administrative machinery developed by most of the state library agencies for the distribution of LSCA funds has remained unchanged, operating in a manner like that of a private foundation. To obtain funds a public library must submit a proposal to its state agency describing a project. Unless the project is innovative or experimental, it has little or no chance for approval. Demonstration, research, and experimentation are the considerations that generally determine whether a project is accepted. Moreover, approval is for a relatively short duration and is usually not renewable. If the project proves to be successful, the library is compelled to continue it with its own funds or abandon it. Thus much of the value to be gained from the project may be lost.

What libraries urgently need are not demonstration projects (however valuable they may be) but funds for books and other materials, and for adequate staff. This would involve a commitment by the federal government to share in the cost of library service; the rationale for this concept will shortly be presented.

Title I of LSCA requires a complete overhauling. As it is now constituted, LSCA is a categorical grant-in-aid program. This type of federal support was tolerable under the Library Services Act of 1956, since it was considered to be a temporary measure. But when LSCA was born in 1964. it was intended to be permanent. The grant-in-aid design has not met the urgent needs of public libraries: it should be recast in a different mold. There is a form of federal assistance referred to as the "per capita general support grant," which is far better suited for a program that has for its purpose the extension and improvement of public-library services. Assistance should be made available to all public libraries rather than a small number, as is now the case. Just as the Elementary and Secondary Education Act under Title IV-B makes federal funds available to every school library, LSCA should likewise provide funds for every public library. Safeguards must be enforced so that neither the state nor its local subdivisions are permitted to lower existing levels of support. In fact, federal legislation should be so designed as to provide incentives for the establishment and expansion of state-aid programs for public libraries.

The per capita general-support-grant principle, which would give direct federal assistance to all public libraries, would compensate for disparities in the amount of taxable wealth among the states. An equilization factor can be designed so as to provide poorer states with a larger pro rata share of the funds. Furthermore, this is a mobile nation. More than a million people move from one state to another every year. It is desirable from a social and political viewpoint that the level of public-library service be equalized so that people are not penalized when they move from one state to another. The quality of service should not be dependent on where one is born or where one happens to live. This problem can be ameliorated through direct federal aid.

Our national welfare requires an educated and productive citizenry. Everyone is entitled to have the fullest opportunity to achieve the highest level of attainment that ability and interests will permit. Public libraries are admirably suited to assist in reaching this aim—which is another reason for federal support.

The federal government taps the resources of the entire nation, generating two-thirds of all taxes collected. Yet these funds have not been drawn upon as heavily as potential state and local sources. The increase in the rate of taxation—and in the rate of debt—have been in recent years far greater at the lower levels of government than at the federal. All of this means that the national government is in a better position to provide increased assistance to public libraries.

Finally, it must be emphasized again that public libraries rely heavily on the local property tax for financial support. But the property tax, as already observed, lacks elasticity as compared with the income and sales taxes and is particularly disastrous in periods of high inflation. Two recent developments make it imperative to seek alternative sources of revenue. The first of these is Proposition 13, which first appeared in California but soon spread to other parts of the country. Public libraries have been the first to experience its effects. In 1980 Massachusetts adopted a similar measure, Proposition 2½, which limits property taxes to two and a half percent of full market value of real estate or to 1979 levels if they were lower than two and a half percent. Proposition 2½ requires communities to reduce their taxes by fifteen percent each year until they reach the two and a half percent maximum. More than one hundred municipalities are expected to reduce property taxes as a consequence of this referendum. Public libraries that will be most affected are those in the state's largest, poorest, and oldest cities, whose property tax rates are higher than the limit fixed by the referendum. It is predicted that Boston could lose about seventy-five percent of its property-tax revenues over a few years.

A second development is the series of lawsuits filed across the country seeking to invalidate the present system of financing public education. The legal question is whether the present scheme, with its substantial dependence upon the local property tax and the resultant wide disparities in revenue between school districts, violates the equal-protection clause of the Fourteenth Amendment to the U.S. Constitution. And the same holds true for public-library service.

All of these points make a strong case for the per capita general-support grant as an instrument to be employed by the federal government for direct assistance to public libraries. This approach should supplant the categorical grant-in-aid philosophy inherent in LSCA. A study issued by the National Commission on Libraries and Information Science, *Evaluation of the Effectiveness of Federal Funding of Public Libraries* (page 112), concluded: "It is equally clear that in its present form the Library Services and Construction Act is a deficient mechanism for the distribution of federal funds and a weak instrument of federal policy with respect to library services development."

There are those who take the position that education and library service are matters of concern to state and local rather than the federal government. This idea, however, is a product of the eighteenth and early nineteenth centuries. The industrial revolution of the late nineteenth century in this country and the electronic revolution in information, communication, and transportation of the twentieth century have rendered this concept obsolete. Today it is imperative that the national government be involved in the field of education and library and information services. Under the "welfare clause" of the U.S. Constitution a strong legal case can be made for this position. It should be recalled that a host of social legislation, previously held to be unconstitutional in an earlier period by the U.S. Supreme Court, was later found to be constitutional under the welfare clause during the Franklin Roosevelt era. Moreover, it must be observed again that the federal government has preempted the major sources of tax revenues, and for this reason alone it must become a partner with the states and municipalities in helping to provide the essential services required by American citizens—one of which is definitely library and information services. The next years will determine which philosophy of the role of the federal government prevails.

Proposed National Library Act

The White House Conference on Libraries and Information Services, held in 1979 in Washington, D.C., attempted to deal with almost every issue that faces American librarianship. Although only twenty-five resolutions were officially adopted, many of them were of the omnibus variety, calling attention to the multiplicity of problems that plague the library world. Practically every resolution will require some legislation for its implementation.

Even before the Conference convened, the Urban Libraries Council joined forces with the National Citizens Emergency Committee to Save Our Public Libraries in order to obtain a more favorable federal commitment to public libraries. Both the Council and the Committee believed it essential to develop a new federal legislative program relating to public libraries that could be presented to the delegates of the White House Conference for their consideration and adoption. At their behest Senator Jacob Javits of New York introduced a bill (S. 1124) proposing a National Library Act, which was cosponsored by Edward Kennedy of Massachusetts. Intended as a study bill designed to stimulate discussion at the White House Conference, the bill contained two innovative features: 1/ it provided for the establishment of an independent federal library agency, without, however, designating the branch of government in which it should reside; and 2/ it provided for direct federal assistance to public libraries on a per capita basis for general operating purposes. At the White House Conference the proposed National Library Act received considerable attention from the delegates. After vigorous discussion and debate they approved the bill in principle by adopting a resolution endorsing "a national library act incorporating the general principles, goals and objectives of S. 1124 with such modifications as shall appear desirable after full Congressional hearings."

Subsequent discussion led to revision of the bill, which was reintroduced into the Senate by Jacob Javits in 1980. Under the title National Library and Information Services Act, it was cosponsored by Senators Kennedy (Massachusetts), Randolph (West Virginia), Pell (Rhode Island), Stafford (Vermont), and Williams (New Jersey). This measure incorporates many of the relevant resolutions adopted at the White House Conference. In fact, the *Congressional Record* for June 20, 1980, on page 7644 features an index that makes reference to the various resolutions that were adopted at the White House Conference and that are now part of the proposed legislation.

Objections to this bill have been raised in some quarters on the ground that it is not sufficiently "national" in scope to merit such a designation, because it does not pay adequate attention to school and academic libraries. However, when the bill was drafted, it was the feeling of the major school and academic library organizations that they did not want to be included, preferring instead to be part of the general federal legislation that deals with education.

The bill as drafted does, nevertheless, highlight its national scope. The opening sentence calls on the government to promote universal library and information services. The declaration goes on to state that "it is essential that a national program be established to insure that an adequate level of library and information services is made available in all communities accessible to all residents." Another section makes it clear that this Act is designed to encourage and assist comprehensive planning, coordination, and development of multitype library and information networks. The law defines "network" as "a formal arrangement under which materials, information and services provided by a variety of types of libraries and other organizations are made available to all potential users and is designed to provide for the systematic and effective coordination of the resources of school, public, academic and special libraries and information centers." Moreover, Title I of the Act would provide grants for establishing, expanding, and operating intrastate, statewide, regional, multistate, and national cooperative networks for the systematic and effective coordination of the resources of school, public, academic, and special libraries and information centers, public and private. A substantial portion of the funds appropriated under this Act would have to be employed for interlibrary cooperation and network support.

The National Library and Information Services Act is without a doubt the most ambitious piece of federal library legislation that has been proposed to date. Its scope is broad, touching every type of library. Its reach is national, recognizing more positively than ever before that the federal government should assume a greater role in helping state and local governments to provide adequate library and information services for every citizen in the United States.

Section 7 of the bill would establish an Office of Libraries and Learning Technologies in the Department of Education, to be headed by a Deputy Assistant Secretary. The national dimensions of the proposed activities to be undertaken by the Office are revealed in the following paragraph, which is only one of eighteen designated areas of federal responsibility:

> (2) encourage and assist comprehensive planning, coordination and development of multitype library and information networks and exchange programs, including—
>
> (A) both profit and not-for-profit libraries from the public and private sector.
>
> (B) the Library of Congress.
>
> (C) a national periodicals system, and
>
> (D) a national lending library for print and non-profit materials.
>
> in cooperation with State library agencies and such other agencies, organizations, or libraries as are involved in such networks and programs, except that the operation of such networks shall be controlled at the State or regional level and shall be accessible equally to benefit all individuals.

Because the proposed National Library Act is the most comprehensive legislation conceived to date, it is worth looking further at its provisions. Even if the Act is not passed, this examination will serve to record the essentials of what may not be a model act for national library legislation, but which goes as far as the thinking of political and professional leaders had progressed by the 1980s.

Title I—Interlibrary Cooperation and Network Support

This Title would provide grants for establishing, expanding, and operating intrastate, statewide, regional, multistate, and national cooperative networks of libraries for the systematic and effective coordination of the resources of school, public, academic, and special libraries and information centers, including bibliographic access and the conversion of collections and catalogs to machine-readable data bases. It would also provide special financial assistance for collection maintenance or development for research libraries and major academic libraries that are heavily used by public libraries in the state. The Secretary of Education would be authorized to set aside not more than fifteen percent of the funds under this Title for making discretionary grants to library networks. No library or information center would receive assistance under this Title unless it agreed to share its own resources on a fair and equitable basis with other participating libraries. The bill would authorize $20 million annually for Title I from fiscal year 1983 to 1987.

Title II—Public Library Services

This Title would provide grants for the extension and improvement of public-library services. The state library administrative agency would be required to "distribute funds received under this title directly to the public libraries in that State for general support purposes." Furthermore, Section 203(3) of the Act declares that the state program must set forth the criteria used in allocating funds for the above purpose, which would ensure that the funds are distributed among public libraries on the basis of population "subject to such adjustments as may be provided by reasonable standards and regulations adopted by the State library administrative agency." The bill further provides that any public library receiving funds under this title must share its resources on an exchange basis with other public libraries in the state, and that not more than five percent of the funds received by the state under this Act could be used for meeting federal reporting and compliance requirements. Finally, the bill would authorize appropriations for this purpose.

Title III—Public Library Construction

Grants under this Title would be provided for the construction of public libraries, for their remodeling to meet the standards of the Architectural Barriers Act of 1968 and to conserve energy, and for the acquisition and conversion of existing structures for use as public libraries. The amount authorized for this purpose would be $150 million annually from fiscal 1983 to 1987.

Title IV—Public Library Programs to Meet Special User Needs

Grants under this Title would be made available for the following special user needs: 1/ rural library service; 2/ literacy training for the functionally illiterate; 3/ job-information services and career counseling; 4/ English-language instruction; 5/ library services for the aging and physically handicapped; 6/ extension library services to patients, residents, and inmates of hospitals, correctional facilities, and other publicly supported institutions; 7/ outreach programs to serve the economically and educationally disadvantaged; 8/ technical and reference services to serve business, employee, scientific, or other special groups; 9/ information and referral centers; 10/ library and information services to Indians on reservations; and 11/ library programs developed in cooperation with public agencies and private organizations. The bill would authorize appropriations for this purpose.

Title V—Planning and Development

This Title would provide grants to state library administrative agencies to meet the costs of planning and evaluation, studies and research, and coordination of regional and national networks. It would also disburse grants for a variety of programs, such as in-service training, continuing education, and career-service development for local library personnel. Grants would be available for public-awareness programs designed to promote the use and value of library and information services in meeting the needs of citizens. The bill would authorize appropriations for this purpose.

National Commission on Libraries and Information Science

Another important development in the field of federal library legislation was the establishment of the National Commission on Libraries and Information Science under an act of Congress approved July 20, 1970. This statute contains a noteworthy statement of policy:

> The Congress hereby affirms that library and information services adequate to meet the needs of the people of the United States are essential to achieve national goals and to utilize most effectively the Nation's educational resources and that the Federal Government will cooperate with State and local governments and public and private agencies in assuring optimum provision of such agencies.

The Commission, an independent federal agency within the executive branch of the national government, consists of the Librarian of Congress and fourteen members appointed by the President, five of whom must be professional librarians or information specialists. The functions of the Commission as stated in the Act are as follows:

(1) advise the President and the Congress on library policy;
(2) conduct studies, surveys, and analyses of the library and information needs of the nation;
(3) appraise the adequacies and deficiencies of current library and information resources and services;
(4) develop plans for meeting national library and informational needs and for the coordination of activities of the federal, state, and local levels of government;
(5) advise federal, state, local, and private agencies regarding library and information sciences;
(6) promote research and development activities which will extend and improve the nation's library and information-handling capability;
(7) submit to the President and the Congress an annual report of its activities;
(8) make and publish such additional reports as it deems to be necessary.

The law also authorizes the Commission to contract with federal and other public and private agencies to carry out its functions and to conduct hearings. Finally, the law directs all federal agencies to cooperate with the Commission in carrying out the purposes of the Act.

The Commission orchestrated and was responsible, under an act of Congress, for conducting the White House Conference; it played an important role in promoting the plan and the legislation for a National Periodical Center; and it has commissioned and published a variety of studies and reports that are of great value to American librarianship. As an authorized and funded agency at the national level, it is a strategic link in the evolving federal-state-local legal structure for library service.

Depository-Library System

The depository program is a long-established arrangement under which government publications are supplied free of charge to participating libraries for the purpose of making them more accessible to the American public. The program is administered by the Office of the Superintendent of Documents, which was established in 1895. The practice of permitting each member of the House and Senate to designate a depository library in his or her area was begun in 1857.

At first depository libraries were required to accept and retain all publications offered them. In 1922, however, a plan was adopted that permitted them to select in advance the type of material they desired to receive on a regular basis. The Superintendent of Documents maintains a classified list of the series and groups of publications from which the libraries can make their selections. The list is revised as new categories are made available.

Through the years there has developed three serious defects in this system. First was the need for additional depositories. A century ago the limitation of one for each Congressional district was reasonable. Today, however, with the growth and increasing mobility of the population, this limiting provision has served as a stumbling block.

A second defect resulted from the manner in which government publications came to be produced. Under the law as it existed prior to 1962 only the documents that were actually published at the Government Printing Office were made available to depository libraries—which, up to the time of Franklin Roosevelt, meant *all* of them. The GPO was originally designed to produce materials needed by Congress, and later, by all branches of the federal establishment. But in more recent years it has been physically impossible for the GPO to meet the demands made on it. As a practical solution to this problem the Joint Committee on Printing authorized certain departments and agencies of the government to set up subsidiary field or departmental plants to produce some materials. In 1962 there were three hundred and sixty-two such facilities scattered throughout the United States, with some of them located abroad.

In the years that followed this venture, depository libraries began to complain that they were not receiving the documents issued from the subsidiary presses. The situation became so serious that a number of the major research libraries, through the cooperation of ALA and the Library of Congress, organized an office at the Library—the Documents Expediting Office—whose function it is to obtain for these libraries the publications produced at the subsidiary printing plants.

A third defect in the depository system was the requirement that participating libraries retain all government publications indefinitely; weeding was not permitted. This forced many libraries to curtail their requests for materials that would have been useful only for short periods of time. Even the permanent retention of the vast body of literature that depository libraries selected constituted a real problem, requiring ever-increasing shelf space and staff.

A major revision of the depository system occurred with the passage of the Depository Library Act of 1962, which was further amended in 1968. Under the present law all government publications are available to depository libraries through the facilities of the Superintendent of Documents, except for those documents that are determined by the issuing office to be required for office use only; are required for strictly administrative operational purposes that have no public interest or educational value; or are classified for reasons of national security.

The Act provides that each member of the House of Representatives may designate one additional depository for his or her district, and each senator, one for his or her state. Approximately six hundred new depositories were thus established. Before a new depository library may be designated, however, the applicant must submit a certification, signed by the head of the library, as to the need for such designation. The law also allows for two regional depositories to be set up in each state with special responsibilities assigned to them. These libraries are required to give reference service within the region and to make all government publications available on interlibrary loan. They must also receive and maintain a complete collection of all publications distributed by the Superintendent of Documents.

A significant feature of this law is the provision permitting depository libraries to dispose of government publications that they have retained for at least five years. The problem of distributing documents issued by subsidiary printing plants has not been completely resolved. The law directs the Superintendent of Documents to inform the government agencies that operate subsidiary plants as to the number of copies of their publications that are required for distribution to depository libraries, and provides that the cost of printing the copies to be distributed must be borne by the agency responsible for their issuance.

In September 1979 the National Publications Act of 1979 was introduced in the House of Representatives to provide for improved administration of public printing services and distribution of public documents. The bill, which represents a thoroughgoing revision of the existing law relative to the operation of the Government Printing Office and the Office of the Superintendent of Public Documents, would create an independent establishment in the executive branch of the federal government to be known as the National Publications Agency. Within this agency the law provides for a National Publications Commission of seven members to be appointed by the President, together with the chairman of the Committee on House Administration, the chairman of the Committee on Rules and Administration of the Senate, and the director of the Office of Management and Budget. One of the members would have to be chosen from the library field. The Commission would be responsible for policy direction and overall management and operation of the National Publications Agency.

The proposed law provides further that within the National Publications Agency there is to be a Director of Distribution

Services, responsible for maintenance of a complete collection of public documents; distribution of public documents through the National Publication Agency, including oversight, inspection, and support of depository libraries; and international exchange of public documents in cooperation with the Librarian of Congress and the Archivist of the United States.

There are a number of other provisions of considerable interest to libraries. The law would require that the price at which a public document is offered for sale could not be less than the cost of its production and distribution—except upon a determination by the Commission or the issuing government entity that the public interest so requires. The Director of Distribution Services would be responsible for maintaining a comprehensive cumulative index of public documents, a provision that is not present in the existing law. The National Publications Act may well shortly be enacted into law.

Legal Basis of Federal Libraries

The first federal library was the Library of Congress, although this was not its official name at the time. It was created by a congressional measure entitled "An Act Concerning the Library for the Use of Both Houses of Congress," approved January 26, 1802. The law provided a room in the Capitol, and the President of the Senate and the Speaker of the House were empowered to establish regulations and restrictions for governing the Library. The law also provided that the Librarian was to be appointed by the President of the United States at a salary of not more than $2 "per diem for every day of necessary attendance." Finally, the use of the Library was restricted to the President, Vice-President, and members of Congress.

A few years later the administration of the Library was transferred to a Joint Committee on the Library, consisting of three senators appointed by the President of the Senate and three representatives appointed by the Speaker of the House. This Committee has continued to function to the present day. Since 1947, however, it has consisted of the chairman and four members of the Senate Committee on Rules and Administration and the chairman and four members of the Committee on House Administration.

This meager statute represents the legal basis for the Library of Congress as it exists today—a library with thousands of employees, millions of books and other materials, carrying on a multiplicity of library services and activities in three huge government buildings with an annual budget of almost $200 million. To be sure, there have been other isolated congressional enactments in the intervening years as certain legal exigencies required, but there was no attempt made to formulate a basic or comprehensive statutory foundation that befits a vast institution like the Library of Congress.

The one exception to this generalization relates to the Library's Congressional Research Service, formerly known as the Legislative Reference Service. When the name-change took place, in 1970, Congress drafted a detailed and comprehensive statute that brought up to date all of its legal facets. The law begins with a statement of policy that declares that the Librarian of Congress must in every possible way encourage, assist, and promote the Congressional Research Service. Furthermore, the Librarian is directed to grant and accord the Service complete research independence and the maximum practicable administrative independence consistent with the stated objectives. The Act prescribes the functions and duties of the Service with great detail, enumerating twenty-three broad fields of research. The Librarian of Congress at the recommendation of the director is authorized to appoint specialists in each of these fields and to employ, as needed, experts in other specializations. Finally, the director of the Service is authorized to prepare budget estimates and to submit them to the Librarian of Congress.

It is clear that the Congressional Research Service has a strong legal basis for its operations, but this is not true for the other major functions of the Library. There is a definite need for a thorough revision and expansion of the law governing the Library of Congress. The administrative staff of the Library cannot, of course, assume the initiative in promoting such legislation; it is a task for the National Commission on Libraries and Information Science or the American Library Association.

One must remember that the United States does not have a national library *per se*, even though the Library of Congress performs many of the functions of one. As long as it remains the Library *of Congress*, it cannot fully play the wider role. The idea of a national library for the United States is not a new one. As early as August 28, 1823, the *National Intelligencer*, under the headline "National Library," declared:

> We wish we could promise ourselves to see the day when the Library of Congress should be more than half filled with books of acknowledged excellence, in every branch of science, and collected from every country. We should like it, also, to be something more national and truly literary in its arrangements and objects than it has hitherto been. . . . We do hope that Congress will make such regulations for the increase and utility of this noble institution as will contribute greatly to the improvement of our country, the satisfaction of literary men of leisure who reside near the seat of government, and will increase our respectability in this respect in the eyes of foreign nations. . . . there should be no work of high character and unquestionable utility published in any part of the world which ought not, in time, to find its way into the National Library of the United States.

More than a century later, when Archibald MacLeish was Librarian of Congress, he enunciated a policy of service the scope and dimensions of which were those of a national library. On September 11, 1940, he drafted "Three Canons of Service." The third canon is particularly relevant here:

> 3. The reference staff and facilities of the Library of Congress are available to members of the public, universities, learned societies and other libraries requiring service which the library staff is equipped to give and which can be given without interference with services to the Congress and other agencies of the Federal Government. . . . Actively considered, the Library's policy in this regard means that the Library of Congress, as the reference library of the people, holds itself charged with a duty to

> provide information to the people with regard to the materials they possess in its collections, and with an obligation to make its technical and scholarly services as broadly useful to the people as it can.

With the new electronic technologies that are revolutionizing library techniques and capabilities, this may be the moment when the concept of a National Library of the United States should be actively pursued and realized.

Other Federal Libraries

What about the many other federal libraries? Although they number in the thousands, the basis for their existence, like that of the Library of Congress, rests on very meager legislation. Most have been created through administrative fiat. The only one that has a substantial legal foundation is the National Library of Medicine, established under an act of Congress adopted in 1944. This law begins with a declaration of the library's purpose and proceeds to describe its functions in detail. The statute provides for a board of regents of ten members appointed by the President, together with four ex officio members (including the Librarian of Congress) whose duties are to advise the Secretary of the Department of Health and Human Services on matters of policy relative to the library. It also authorizes the Administrator of General Services to provide adequate building facilities for the library, and grants the Secretary the power to establish regional branches.

There are two other federal libraries to which the term "National Library" has been applied: the National Library of Agriculture and the National Library of Natural Resources of the Department of Interior. Both of these have rich collections and strong staffs, but they lack the benefit of independent congressional enactments to support their legal status. Here, too, the National Commission on Libraries and Information Science or the American Library Association should intervene to ensure that these two important government libraries receive an adequate legislative mandate.

Federal provisions for libraries are incomplete and sometimes unclear with regard both to service in the federal establishment itself and to the role of the national government in library service across the nation. The house has been built piecemeal and not from an overall plan, and as a result it has neither the rooms nor the integration of space required in a modern structure.

IX SPECIAL LEGAL PROBLEMS OF CONCERN TO LIBRARIES

SEVERAL bodies of law, though not limited to libraries, nonetheless have a direct impact on them. Most important are copyright, security of property, freedom of expression, and the right to privacy. In these matters libraries are subject to general legislation and adjudication that go beyond library considerations and that may at times go counter to library interests.

Copyright

A new national Copyright Act became effective on January 1, 1978. The first major revision of the law since 1909, it contains a number of basic changes of concern to libraries.

One of these is the abolition of common-law copyright under Section 301 of the Act. Instead of a dual system of common-law copyright for unpublished works and statutory copyright for published works, which had been in effect since 1790, the new act adopts a single system of statutory copyright from the date of the creation of the work. As a result authors now commonly add a copyright notice as soon as a manuscript is completed, thus giving it protection under law prior to publication.

Another fundamental change in the law is that the doctrine of fair use, developed by judicial decisions through the years, is given statutory recognition for the first time, in Section 107. The law does not define fair use, but it does specify certain purposes falling within the concept, such as "criticism, comment, news reporting, teaching (including multiple copies for classroom use), scholarship or research." The law also sets forth the following factors to be included in determining whether the use made of a work in any particular case is "fair": 1/ the purpose and character of the use, including whether such use is of a commercial nature or is for nonprofit educational purposes; 2/ the nature of the copyrighted work; 3/ the amount and substantiality of the portion used in relation to the copyrighted work as a whole; and 4/ the effect of the use upon the potential market or value of the copyrighted work.

The doctrine of fair use was designed by the courts to balance the right of the public's access to knowledge with the right of authors to protection of their creations. Although the courts have ruled over and over again upon the fair-use doctrine, no concrete definition has ever been produced, since by its nature it is an equitable rule of reason. Each case raising this issue of law must be decided on its own facts. However, the courts in their cumulative decisions have identified certain criteria by which the doctrine of fair use can be applied. These criteria have been reduced to standards by the drafters of the new law and have been incorporated into Section 107.

Another important innovation in the law is Section 108, which spells out the rights of reproduction and distribution of a work by libraries and archives. These rights may be summarized as follows:

(a) It is not an infringement of copyright for a library or archives to reproduce or distribute no more than one copy of a work, providing (1) it is made without any direct or indirect commercial advantage; (2) the collections are open to the public, or available not only to researchers affiliated with the library or archives, or with the institution of which it is a part, but also to other persons doing research in a specialized field; (3) the reproduction includes a notice of copyright.

(b) The rights of reproduction and distribution apply to an unpublished work, duplicated solely for purposes of preservation and security or for deposit for research use in another library.

(c) The right of reproduction applies to a copy of a published work duplicated for the purpose of replacement of a copy that is damaged, deteriorated, lost or stolen, if the library or archives has determined, after a reasonable effort, that an unused copy cannot be obtained at a fair price.

(d) The rights of reproduction and distribution apply to a copy, made from the collection of a library or archives where an individual user or another library or archives requests a copy of no more than one article from a copyrighted collective work or periodical issue, or to a copy of a small part of any other copyrighted work. This is permitted, if the copy becomes the property of the user and the library or archives and the library or archives has had no notice that the copy would be used for any other purpose than private study, scholarship or research. The law also requires that the library or archives displays prominently, at the place where orders for reproduction are accepted as well as on its order form, a warning of copyright.

(e) The rights of reproduction and distribution apply to the entire work or to a substantial part of it made from the collection of a library or archives, if the latter has first determined that a copy of a copyrighted work cannot be obtained at a fair price. This is also subject to the two restrictions mentioned in (d) above.

(f) Nothing in Section 108:
(1) shall be construed to impose liability for copyright infringement upon a library or archives or its employees for the unsupervised use of reproducing equipment located on its premises, if such equipment displays a warning of copyright; (2) excuses a person who uses such equipment from liability of copyright infringement, if he or she exceeds fair use; (3) shall be construed to limit reproduction and distribution of a limited number of copies by a library or archives of an audiovisual news program; or (4) in any way affects the right of fair use or any contractual obligations assumed by the library or archives when it obtained a copy of a work in its collections.

(g) The same material may be reproduced on separate and unrelated occasions by a library or archives, providing it is not engaged in "systematic reproduction." The law does not define "systematic reproduction." However, it does state that nothing prevents a library or archives from participating in interlibrary loan arrangements, providing that the library or archives receiving the reproductions for distribution does not do so in such aggregate quantities as to substitute for a subscription to or purchase of the work.

(h) The rights of reproduction and distribution under Section 108 do not apply to a musical work, a pictorial, graphic or sculptural work, or a motion picture or other audiovisual work other than one dealing with news.

(i) Five years from the effective date of the Copyright Act and at five-year intervals thereafter, the Register of Copyrights shall submit to the Congress a report setting forth the extent to which Section 108 has achieved the intended statutory balance in meeting the rights of creators and the needs of library users, and to make other recommendations.

To assist in interpreting some of the language of Section 108 the House-Senate conference committee on the new copyright law included in its final report a letter from the National Commission on New Technological Uses of Copyrighted Works (CONTU). This communication contains guidelines spelling out the meaning of some of the provisions of Section 108. Although these guidelines do not have the force of law, the conference committee agreed that they are a reasonable interpretation of the provisions in question. They declare that the words "such aggregate quantities as to substitute for a subscription to or purchase of such work" shall mean the following:

(a) With respect to any given periodical (as opposed to any given issue of a periodical) filled requests of a library or archives (a "requesting entity") within any calendar year for a total of six or more copies of an article or articles published in such periodical within five years prior to the date of the request.

(b) With respect to any other material described in subsection 108(d) (including fiction and poetry) filled requests of a requesting entity within any calendar year for a total of six or more copies or phonorecords of or from any given work (including a collective work) during the entire period when such material shall be protected by a copyright.[29]

The CONTU guidelines also require that the requesting entity maintains records of all of its requests for copies or phonorecords of any materials to which these guidelines apply. It must, moreover, maintain records of the fulfillment of such requests and retain them until the end of the third complete calendar year. Finally, provision is made for the review of the CONTU guidelines not later than five years from the effective date of the Act.

The House-Senate conference committee report also called attention to an issue that had arisen as to the meaning of the phrase "audiovisual news program." The Committee declared that a library or archives would be free to reproduce on videotape, or any other medium of fixation or reproduction, local, regional, or network newscasts, interviews concerning current news events, and on-the-spot coverage of news events, and to distribute a limited number of reproductions of such a program on a loan basis.

The problem of classroom photocopying by teachers and school librarians was also given special consideration by the House Judiciary Subcommittee that was responsible for drafting the new copyright law. On its initiative, educators, authors, and publishers reached an agreement that sets forth guidelines for classroom copying in not-for-profit educational institutions regarding books and periodicals. The guidelines, recognized, like those of CONTU, as a reasonable interpretation of fair use by the Subcommittee, state the minimum and not the maximum standards of educational fair use under the new Act. The parties agreed that the conditions determining the extent of permissable copying may change; certain types of copying permitted under the guidelines may be forbidden in the future, and certain types now forbidden may be allowed. The parties also agreed that the guidelines are not intended to limit the types of copying permitted under the standards of fair use under judicial decision, and that there may be instances in which copying that does not fall within the guidelines may nevertheless be permitted under the criteria of fair use as stated in Section 107.

The guidelines provide the following:

I *Single Copying for Teachers*

A single copy may be made of any of the following by or for a teacher at his or her individual request for his or her scholarly research use or use in teaching or preparation to teach a class:

A. A chapter from a book;

B. An article from a periodical or newspaper;
C. A short story, short essay or short poem, whether or not from a collective work;
D. A chart, graph, diagram, drawing, cartoon or picture from a book, periodical, or newspaper.

II *Multiple Copies for Classroom Use*

Multiple copies (not to exceed in any event more than one copy per pupil in a course) may be made by or for the teacher giving the course for classroom use or discussion; provided that:

A. The copying meets the tests of brevity and spontaneity as defined below; and
B. Meets the cumulative effect test as defined below; and
C. Each copy includes a notice of copyright.

[*The various tests referred to above are too detailed to reproduce here but they are contained in the guidelines.*]

III *Prohibitions as to I and II Above*

Notwithstanding any of the above, the following shall be prohibited:

A. Copying shall not be used to create or to replace or substitute for anthologies, compilations or collected works. . . .
B. There shall be no copying of or from works intended to be "consumable" in the course of study or of teaching. These include workbooks, exercises, standardized tests and test booklets and answer sheets and like consumable material.
C. Copying shall not:
    (a) substitute for the purchase of books, publishers' reprints or periodicals;
    (b) be directed by higher authority;
    (c) be repeated with respect to the same item by the same teacher from term to term.
D. No charge shall be made to the student beyond the actual cost of the photocopying.[30]

Section 108 requires that a "Warning of Copyright" be prominently displayed at the place where orders for photocopies of copyright material are accepted by a library or archives and must also appear on order forms.

The warning under the rules and regulations of the Copyright Office must read as follows:

NOTICE
WARNING OF COPYRIGHT RESTRICTIONS

THE COPYRIGHT LAW OF THE UNITED STATES (TITLE 17, UNITED STATES CODE) GOVERNS THE MAKING OF PHOTOCOPIES OR OTHER REPRODUCTIONS OF COPYRIGHTED MATERIAL.

UNDER CERTAIN CONDITIONS SPECIFIED IN THE LAW, LIBRARIES AND ARCHIVES ARE AUTHORIZED TO FURNISH A PHOTOCOPY OR OTHER REPRODUCTION. ONE OF THESE SPECIFIED CONDITIONS IS THAT THE PHOTOCOPY OR REPRODUCTION IS NOT TO BE "USED FOR ANY PURPOSE OTHER THAN PRIVATE STUDY, SCHOLARSHIP OR RESEARCH." IF A USER MAKES A REQUEST FOR, OR LATER USES, A PHOTOCOPY OR REPRODUCTION FOR PURPOSES IN EXCESS OF "FAIR USE," THAT USER MAY BE LIABLE FOR COPYRIGHT INFRINGEMENT.

THIS INSTITUTION RESERVES THE RIGHT TO REFUSE TO ACCEPT A COPYING ORDER, IF IN ITS JUDGMENT, FULFILLMENT OF THE ORDER WOULD INVOLVE VIOLATION OF COPYRIGHT LAW.[31]

The regulations require that this warning be printed on heavy paper in type at least 18 points in size.

Another significant change in the new Act is the duration of copyright. Section 302 provides that copyright in a work created after January 1, 1978, subsists from the date of its creation and endures for a term consisting of the life of the author and fifty years after the author's death. In the case of a "work for hire," which is defined as a "work prepared by an employee within the scope of his or her employment," the copyright endures for a term of seventy-five years from the year of its publication, or a term of one hundred years from the year of its creation, whichever expires first. Section 303 provides that copyright in a work created before January 1, 1978, but not thereafter in the public domain or copyrighted, subsists from January 1, 1978, and endures for the term provided in Section 302. In no case, however, can the term of copyright in such a work expire before December 31, 2002. If the work is published on or before December 31, 2002, the term of copyright will not expire before December 31, 2027. Since the effective date of the new law is January 1, 1978, the term of works copyrighted prior to that is governed by the old law.

With respect to copyright infringement Section 504 provides that if the infringer is an employee or agent of a nonprofit educational institution, library, or archives acting within the scope of his or her employment, there is no liability for statutory damages if such infringer believed and had reasonable grounds for believing that his or her use of the copyrighted work was a fair use under Section 107.

Librarians who are in charge of special collections have raised the question of whether the fair-use doctrine applies to unpublished materials. There is today no definitive answer to this question; all of the case law involving fair use deals with published works. However, after carefully examining the new Act, one can conclude that fair use does apply to an unpublished work. The present law affords it the same legal protection as published material (Section 301): copyright protection from the date of creation through the author's lifetime and fifty years thereafter. Furthermore, both unpublished and published work may be registered in the Copyright Office by depositing a copy, thus affording the copyright holder additional protection (Section 408). It can therefore be argued that since an unpublished work has the same legal protection as a published work, it should also be subject to the same limitations, one of which is fair use.

It should also be pointed out that Section 107 of the Act, which deals with fair use, makes no distinction between published and unpublished materials. Moreover, unpublished works receive copyright protection upon creation; it follows that it was the intention of Congress to make fair use applicable to them—otherwise Section 107 would have been drafted to exclude them.

Section 108(b) of the Act reads as follows: "The rights of reproduction under the section apply to a copy or phonorecord of an unpublished work duplicated in facsimile form solely for the purposes of preservation and security or for deposit for research use in another library or archives." Here again it would appear that it was the intention of Congress to make an unpublished work subject to fair use; otherwise the words "for deposit for research use" in the above context would be meaningless, since "research use" cannot be implemented without fair use. It follows that a library may make an unpublished work available to students and scholars for research purposes without incurring legal liability, providing there have been no restrictions stipulated by the donor.

Users, however, must be made aware in some concrete fashion that the unpublished work they are using is protected under the copyright law and that they cannot publish or distribute it. An unpublished work may lack a visible notice of copyright, and it is imperative that the librarian notify users that it is in fact under copyright protection. The warning notice may be stamped on, or attached to, the work itself. It is also possible to have a form that could cover the entire manuscript collection. This would be signed by all users—acknowledgment that they are aware of the notice of copyright. As an added protection the form should contain a statement that the user will indemnify and hold harmless the library against all suits, claims, actions, and expenses arising from use of the collection.

A number of other questions relating to the transfer of the ownership of copyright are of interest to libraries, particularly those with manuscript collections. Does the gift of an unpublished work automatically transfer the ownership of copyright in that work to the donee? The answer is no. Section 202 provides that ownership of a copyright, or any of the exclusive rights under a copyright, is distinct from ownership of any material object in which the work is embodied. Thus transfer of ownership of a manuscript does not convey any rights in the copyrighted work embodied in it. For this reason, it is highly desirable to request the donor of material to transfer the ownership of copyright to the library as well.

How is a transfer of copyright achieved? Section 201(d) provides that the ownership of a copyright may be transferred in whole or in part by means of a conveyance or by operation of law, and may be bequeathed by will or pass as personal property by the applicable laws of intestate succession. Section 204(a) states that the instrument of conveyance must be in writing and signed by the owner of the copyright or a duly authorized agent. This transfer of copyright is revocable. Section 203(3) provides that a termination of a transfer of copyright may be effected at any time during a period of five years beginning at the end of thirty-five years from the date of the execution of the grant.

On January 28, 1981, the Copyright Office held public hearings in Washington to review the extent to which Section 108, dealing with reproductions by libraries, has achieved the intended statutory balance between the needs of creators and those of library users. Robert Wedgeworth, executive director of the American Library Association, was one of the witnesses. These are his conclusions as presented at the hearings:

> (1) There is no evidence that the law, in most cases, is failing adequately to balance the interests of creators and users of copyrighted materials.
> (2) Most photocopying done by or in libraries falls within the protections of fair use and of Section 108 of the law.
> (3) There is no evidence of a causal link between any reductions in library periodical subscriptions and library photocopying practices.
> (4) Libraries may utilize rights under both Sections 107 and 108 to contribute to the widest possible dissemination of information to the public and to fulfill their traditional role in society as lenders and facilitators of such information.
> (5) Librarians are complying with the law and any lack of use of the CCC does not indicate the contrary, but merely reflects the fact that most photocopying done in libraries is within the bounds of Sections 107 and 108.
> (6) Publishers should not view librarians as the "enemy" in a war over photocopy profits. Libraries do not reduce the size of their collections because of the availability of photocopies. Indeed, reliance on networking to substitute for a subscription to a periodical is not only illegal; it is inefficient and expensive. Every library strives to be as comprehensive in its collection development area as it can be. The availability of photocopies for the occasional user interested in an unusual field makes possible the kind of

access to information so important to our society's very foundation.

(7) Since the purpose of the copyright law in rewarding publishers and authors is to stimulate creation and dissemination of intellectual works, statutory provisions should not be interpreted to impede dissemination and access if the stimulus to creation is not thereby augmented. It is doubtful that authors would in any way benefit from any further restriction on access to information in photocopied form.

(8) Librarians are neither administratively equipped, nor should they be required to police their patron's photocopying activities.

(9) The CONTU Guidelines are useful guides, but they do not carry the force of law. The Guidelines do not purport to set maximum limits on library photocopying practices but strive only to establish a safe harbour. They should not be allowed to become firm rules which may cause librarians unnecessarily to deny their patron's rights.

(10) No new restrictions are needed at this time. Certainly no changes in the law or additional guidelines should be considered prior to the completion of the 5-year review and the compilation of data and other evidence clearly demonstrating a need for such restrictions. If anything, a clarification of the unique applicability of the Section 107 fair use factors to address the special concerns of college and university library patrons would be justified.

As of this writing the new copyright provisions appear to be functioning without undue restriction of access to recorded knowledge through libraries. However, every librarian should be familiar with the law, and because copyright is a volatile field, should follow future hearings on the legislation and any changes in it.

Library Security

In recent years the theft of library materials has reached such serious proportions that special legislation has been enacted in a number of states to combat it. Virginia was the first state to adopt a law specifically designed to attempt to curb library theft. The Virginia statute passed in 1975 has two basic provisions the first of which reads as follows:

> Whoever, without authority, with the intention of converting to his own or another's use, willfully conceals a book or other library property, while still on the premises of such library, or willfully without authority removes any book or other property from any of the above libraries or collections shall be deemed guilty of larceny thereof, and upon conviction thereof, shall be punished as provided by law. Proof of the willful concealment of such book or other library property while still on the premises of such library shall be prima facie evidence of intent to commit larceny thereof [*Code of Virginia*, Section 42.7-73].

This provision is unique because it makes the willful concealment of a book or other library property a separate and distinct offense. Furthermore, proof of such concealment constitutes *prima facie* evidence of intent to commit larceny. An individual who conceals a book, for example, with intent to convert it to his or her own use, and is apprehended, will be presumed to have committed larceny. Under these circumstances the burden of proof shifts to the offender to demonstrate that he or she did not intend to commit larceny.

The second basic provision in the Virginia law is a new one:

> A library or agent or employee of the library causing the arrest of any person pursuant to the provision of 42. 1-73, shall not be held civilly liable for unlawful detention, slander, malicious prosecution, false imprisonment, false arrest, or assault and battery of the person so arrested, whether such arrest takes place on the premises of the library or after close pursuit from such premises by such agent or employee; provided that, in causing the arrest of such person, the library or agent or employee of the library had at the time of such arrest probable cause to believe that the person committed willful concealment of books or other library property [*Code of Virginia*, Sec. 1-73.1].

This new approach to library theft was borrowed from the law relating to shoplifting. Under the common law, as distinguished from statutory law, the owner of property was permitted to use reasonable force to recover goods that had been unlawfully taken. But if an innocent person was detained or arrested, his or her remedy was to sue the owner for false arrest, false imprisonment, malicious prosecution, assault and battery, or defamation, depending on the circumstances. Thus the common law did not really provide the merchant with an effective remedy against shoplifting.

The increase in shoplifting that followed World War II made it necessary to design some type of special legislation. As a result almost every state has enacted what is referred to as the shoplifting statute, which contains three basic elements: 1/ it defines the crime of shoplifting as the willful concealment of merchandise with the intention of converting it to one's use; 2/ it authorizes the merchant or an employee to detain the suspect, where there is probable cause to believe that the suspect has committed theft; 3/ it provides the merchant with a legal defense in civil actions arising out of such detention. The shoplifting law makes pilfering a separate and distinct crime by defining it as "willfully concealing any merchandise with the intention of converting it to one's use without payment to the owner." Some of the laws, however, are broader and provide that the finding of merchandise concealed upon a person is *prima facie* evidence of willful concealment. Thus the intent to convert to one's use does not have to be proven by the prosecution. The burden of proof shifts to the accused person to demonstrate that he or she did not intend to steal the merchandise.

The second element in shoplifting legislation is the authorization to detain a suspect when a merchant has probable cause to believe that the suspect has committed the crime of shoplifting. But here one must balance the merchant's right of property with the equally important right of the individual to be free and unmolested. How does the shoplifting statute resolve this dilemma? In the first place, many of the state statutes provide that the merchant must have probable cause to believe that the person detained has committed the crime. The legal test of what constitutes probable cause cannot be determined with mathematical precision. The courts rely heavily on what is known as the "reasonable man" doctrine, which defines probable cause as a suspicion founded on circumstances sufficiently strong to warrant a reasonable person to believe that the charge is true (Sebastion v. Crowley, 38 Cal. App. 2d 194). In addition, many of the statutes provide that the detention of a suspect is permissable only for certain prescribed purposes.

The third element in the shoplifting statute is a provision that grants the merchant immunity from civil liability arising out of the detention of a suspect. The actions for which immunity is granted are generally false arrest, false imprisonment, unlawful detention, assault, battery, slander, and malicious prosecution.

In 1977 the present author drafted "A Model Law Relating to Library Theft," which utilizes the three basic elements found in the shoplifting statute; the model appears as Appendix II. After it was published,[32] several states—California, Ohio, and South Carolina—enacted legislation that is based essentially on the model law. In California the provisions were incorporated into the existing shoplifting statute. Several additional states have the model act under consideration.

Freedom of Expression

The right to free expression is guaranteed to all citizens by the First Amendment to the U.S. Constitution. A corollary to this right is the freedom to read. One cannot exist without the other. But there are those who would deny others both of these freedoms—and libraries are particularly vulnerable to attack. The legal question is whether all forms of expression—oral, written, printed, pictorial—are protected under the First Amendment. In our system of government the courts are the final arbiters in controversies that arise in defining the limits of these vital freedoms. How have they dealt with this problem?

An important case in this area is Roth v. United States (354 U.S. 476), a 1957 decision representing the beginning of the U.S. Supreme Court's struggle with obscenity legislation. Roth conducted a business in New York that engaged in the publication and sale of books, photographs, and magazines. He was convicted by a jury of mailing obscene circulars and advertising an obscene book, in violation of the federal obscenity statute. He appealed to the Supreme Court. In the same proceedings the court also heard the case of *Alberts v. California*, in which the defendant had been convicted for selling obscene and indecent books in violation of the California Penal Code.

Justice Brennan, in writing the majority opinion, began with a review of the question of whether obscenity falls within the area of protected speech and press under the First Amendment. His conclusion was that it was not protected because it was without redeeming social importance. He wrote:

> All ideas having the slightest redeeming social importance—unorthodox ideas, controversial ideas, even ideas hateful to the prevailing climate of opinion—have the full protection of the guaranties unless excludable because they approach upon the limited area of more important interests. But implicit in the history of the First Amendment is the rejection of obscenity as utterly without redeeming social importance. . . . We hold that obscenity is not within the area of constitutionally protected speech or press.

Brennan did not define obscenity. He based his decision on the tests employed in previous rulings of the courts: whether to the average person, applying community standards, the dominant theme of the material taken as a whole appeals to prurient interest. Brennan was satisfied that both of the trial courts below sufficiently followed the proper standard for defining obscenity. He went on to quote from the trial judge's instructions to the jury in the Roth case:

> The test in each case is the effect of the book, picture or publication considered as a whole, not upon any particular class, but upon all those whom it is likely to reach. In other words, you determine its impact upon the average person in the community. The books, pictures and circulars must be judged as a whole, in their entire context, and you are not to consider detached or separate portions in reaching a conclusion. You judge the circulars, pictures and publications which have been put in evidence by present-day standards of the community. You may ask yourselfs does it offend the common conscience of the community by present-day standards.

> In this case, ladies and gentlemen of the jury, you and you alone are the exclusive judges of what the common conscience of the community is, and in determining that conscience you are to consider the community as a whole, young and old, educated and uneducated, the religious and irreligious—men, women and children.

On the basis of the test applied to obscenity in this case, the Supreme Court upheld the conviction of the lower court.

Justice Douglas, however, wrote a dissenting opinion, with which Justice Black concurred, rejecting the test for obscenity on which the majority opinion was based. He wrote:

> I can understand (and at times even sympathize) with programs of civic groups and church groups to protect and defend the existing moral standards of the community. I can understand the motives of the Anthony Comstocks who would impose Victorian standards on the community. When speech alone is involved, I do not think that government, consistently with the First Amendment, can become the sponsor of any of these movements. . . . Government should be concerned with anti-social conduct, not with utterances. Thus, if the First Amendment guarantee of freedom of speech and press is to mean anything in this field, it must allow protests even against the moral code that the standard of the day sets for the community. In other words, literature should not be suppressed merely because it offends the moral code of the censor.

Finally, he declared:

> Freedom of expression can be suppressed if, and to the extent that, it is so closely brigaded with illegal action as to be an inseparable part of it. . . . As a people we cannot afford to relax that standard. For the test that suppresses a cheap tract today can suppress a literary gem tomorrow. All it need do is to incite a lascivious thought or arouse a lustful desire. The list of books that judges or juries can place in that category is endless. I would give the broad sweep of the First Amendment full support. I have the same confidence in the ability of our people to reject noxious literature as I have in their capacity to sort out the true from the false in theology, economics, politics or any other field.

In 1973, in the case of Miller v. California (413 U.S. 15), the Supreme Court revised the test for obscenity inherent in the Roth decision. In this case the defendant was convicted of mailing unsolicited obscene materials in violation of a California statute. The Supreme Court upheld the conviction in a five-to-four decision, with Justice Burger delivering the majority opinion. Burger in general employed the test enunciated in the Roth case. However, he instituted a major change in one of the elements of the test relative to the term "community standards." Heretofore when this term was applied, it was meant to be a national standard and not a local community standard. Justice Burger rejected this view, stating: "To require a state to structure proceedings around evidence of a national 'community standard' would be an exercise in futility."

Justice Douglas filed a dissenting opinion, as did Justice Brennan. Douglas continued his attack, writing, "The Court has worked hard to define obscenity and concededly has failed." He went on to declare:

> Today the Court retreats from the earlier formulations of the constitutional test and undertakes to make new definitions. This effort, like the earlier ones, is earnest and well intentioned. The difficulty is that we do not deal with constitutional terms, since "obscenity" is not mentioned in the Constitution or Bill of Rights. And the First Amendment makes no exception. . . . So there are no constitutional guidelines for deciding what is and what is not "obscene."

On the same day that this decision was rendered the Supreme Court disposed of another obscenity case, Paris Adult Theatre I v. Slaton, (413 U.S. 49). The decision again was five to four, with the same lineup as in the previous case. No new ground was broken. Justice Douglas in a footnote to his dissenting opinion issued the following warning:

> What we do today is rather ominous as respects librarians. The net now designed by the Court is so finely meshed that, taken literally, it could result in raids on libraries. Libraries, I had always assumed, were sacrosanct, representing every part of the spectrum. If what is offensive to the most influential person or

> group in a community can be purged from a library, the library system would be destroyed.

On the basis of those two five-to-four decisions it seems apparent that the Supreme Court is very closely divided on the obscenity issue. Whereas in 1957 Justice Brennan wrote the majority opinion in which he declared that obscenity is not protected under the First Amendment, we find that in 1973 he rendered a dissenting opinion on this question, in which he stated, "Our experience with the *Roth* approach has certainly taught us that the outright suppression of obscenity cannot be reconciled with the fundamental principles of the First and Fourteenth amendments." It is clear that the law on obscenity continues to evolve, and that the social mores of a particular period are reflected in the decisions of the courts.

Practically every state, as well as the federal government, has a law on its statute books making it a criminal offense to sell, distribute, or advertise obscene materials. However, libraries and other scientific and educational institutions are expressly exempt from the operation of such a law in a number of the states. Where such an exemption does not prevail, it seems highly desirable for the state library association to promote its adoption.

We turn now to the principle of freedom of expression as it relates to political, social, and scientific literature. As with obscenity, the Supreme Court has struggled with the legal issues involved in this area of expression. One of the early cases is Schenck v. United States (249 U.S. 47), decided in 1919. Schenck, who was secretary of the Socialist Party, was charged with conspiring to violate the Espionage Act of 1917 by sending through the mail a leaflet that urged men to evade the draft of World War I. The defendant pleaded the First Amendment but was found guilty of the charges, and the case was appealed to the U.S. Supreme Court. Justice Holmes in a relatively brief opinion affirmed the judgment of the lower court. It is in this case that Holmes issued that oft-repeated dictum: "The most stringent protection of free speech would not protect a man in falsely shouting fire in a theater and causing a panic." He went on to elaborate:

> The question in every case is whether the words used are used in such circumstances and are of such a nature as to create a clear and present danger that they will bring about the substantive evils that Congress has a right to prevent. It is a question of proximity and degree. When a nation is at war many things that might be said in peace are such a hindrance to its effort that their utterance will not be endured so long as men fight, and that no court could regard them as protected by any constitutional right.

The next case of considerable importance in this field is Gitlow v. New York (268 U.S. 652), adjudicated in 1925. Here the defendant was indicted under the statutory crime of criminal anarchy in the state of New York. Gitlow was business manager of *Revolutionary Age,* the official organ of the left wing of the Socialist Party. In the first issue a "Manifesto" was published advocating the necessity of accomplishing the "Communist Revolution" through mass industrial revolts for the purpose of ushering in "a revolutionary dictatorship of the proletariat." Counsel for the defendant insisted that the New York statute violated the due-process clause of the Fourteenth Amendment. The state courts, however, rejected this argument and found the defendant guilty, whereupon the case moved to the U.S. Supreme Court. The majority opinion, written by Justice Sanford, affirmed the conviction:

> Manifestly, the legislature has authority to forbid the advocacy of a doctrine designed and intended to overthrow the government without waiting until there is a present and imminent danger of the success of the plan advocated. If the state were compelled to wait until the apprehended danger became certain, then its right to protect itself would come into being simultaneously with the overthrow of the government, when there would be neither prosecuting officers nor courts for the enforcement of the law. We cannot hold that the present statute is an arbitrary or unreasonable exercise of the police power of the state, unwarrantably infringing the freedom of speech or press; and we must and do sustain its constitutionality.

Justice Holmes entered a dissenting opinion, in which Justice Brandeis joined. Holmes based his opinion on the clear-

and-present-danger test enunciated in the Schenck case. He wrote:

> It is said that this Manifesto was more than a theory, that it was an incitement. Every idea is an incitement. It offers itself for belief, and, if believed, it is acted on unless some other belief outweighs it, or some failure of energy stifles the movement at its birth. . . . But whatever may be thought of the redundant discourse before us, it had no chance of starting a present conflagration. If, in the long run, the beliefs expressed in proletarian dictatorship are destined to be accepted by the dominant forces of the community, the only meaning of free speech is that they should be given their chance and have their way.

In Whitney v. California (274 U.S. 375), decided in 1927, Justice Brandeis produced a classic statement on behalf of freedom of expression:

> Those who won our independence believed that the final end of the state was to make men free to develop their faculties; and that in its government the deliberative forces should prevail over the arbitrary. They valued liberty both as an end and as a means. They believed liberty to be the secret of happiness and courage to be the secret of liberty. They believed that freedom to think as you will and to speak as you think are means indispensable to the discovery and spread of political truth; that without free speech and assembly discussion would be futile; that with them, discussion affords ordinarily adequate protection against the dissemination of noxious doctrine; that the greatest menace to freedom is an inert people; and that this should be a fundamental principle of the American government. They recognized the risks to which all human institutions are subject. But they knew that order cannot be secured merely through fear of punishment for its infraction; that it is hazardous to discourage thought, hope and imagination; that fear breeds repression; that repression breeds hate; that hate menaces stable government; that the path of safety lies in the opportunity to discuss freely supposed grievances and proposed remedies; and the fitting remedy for evil counsels is good ones. Believing in the power of reason through public discussion, they eschewed silence coerced by law—the

> argument of force in its worst form. Recognizing the occasional tyrannies of governing majorities, they amended the Constitution so that free speech and assembly should be guaranteed.

Reference must be made to one final case, Brandenburg v. Ohio (395 U.S. 444), decided in 1969. Here the defendant was convicted under the Ohio Criminal Syndicalism statute for advocating crime, violence, and sabotage to achieve industrial and political reform. The defendant was charged with staging a Ku Klux Klan rally at which incendiary speeches were made against blacks and Jews. The conviction was appealed to the Supreme Court. In a unanimous opinion the court overruled the decision of the Ohio courts, stating that a statute that by its own words purports to punish mere advocacy falls within the condemnation of the First and Fourteenth Amendments. The Court also overturned its earlier decision in *Whitney v. California*.

Justice Douglas felt it necessary to deliver a concurring opinion in which he condemned the use of the clear-and-present-danger test. He wrote: "I see no place in the regime of the First Amendment for any 'clear and present danger test'. . . . The line between what is permissable and not subject to control and what may be made impermissable and subject to regulation is the line between ideas and overt acts."

From this brief analysis of the law concerning freedom of expression it may be concluded that the court decisions depend to a large extent on the philosophical predilections of the nine judges who sit on the U.S. Supreme Court bench, and the social and political climate of the country at a given time.

Right of Privacy

The right of privacy also presents legal problems for libraries, particularly for those with manuscript collections of letters, diaries, and case records. This right cannot be easily defined; it is a relatively new legal concept having no previous existence under the common law. The right of privacy has been defined as the right of people to be "let alone" and to be free from unwarranted publicity regarding their personal affairs.

In order for the right of privacy to be involved, the matter that is made public must be one that would be offensive and objectionable to a reasonable person of ordinary sensibilities. Moreover, the right is a personal one and may be enforced only by the person whose right has been infringed; it does not extend to family members unless their own privacy is invaded. The individual right of privacy that any person enjoys during his or her lifetime dies with the person.

To protect the library from possible lawsuits researchers should be required to sign an agreement that they will hold harmless and indemnify the library for any loss or damages resulting from the use of manuscript materials.

The right of privacy is also involved in the handling of library registration and circulation records. In 1978 the state of Florida adopted an act declaring all registration and circulation records of every public library (except general statistical reports of registration and circulation) to be confidential records. No person is permitted to reveal any information in these records except under a proper judicial order. Under this law the term "registration records" includes any information that a library requires a patron to provide in order to become eligible to borrow books and other materials. The term "circulation records" includes all information that identifies the patrons' borrowing of particular books and materials. Finally, the law provides that any person violating its provisions is guilty of a misdemeanor of the second degree.

All state jurisdictions should consider adopting similar legislation.

* * *

In conclusion, it should be noted that library law, like law in general, is a continuous and ongoing process. It is in a constant state of adoption and revision as new legislation is proposed and old legislation revised. It changes with the needs of society. From the foregoing account the examples of copyright and obscenity come immediately to mind. On a broader scale, with the revised concept of federalism, the whole panoply of national legislation for libraries may change.

Consequently it is the duty of librarians to "keep up" with the law, even as they follow the sweep of national and social events. Further, it is the duty of the library profession to keep abreast of social trends and to initiate and promote the type of legislation that will best satisfy the needs of both those who use libraries and those who are responsible for providing library services. The libraries of this country can be effective instruments for enriching the lives of people, but only if they are based on strong legal foundations.

APPENDIX A

A MODEL METROPOLITAN-AREA LIBRARY AUTHORITY ACT

Sec. 1. Short Title: This Act shall be known and may be cited as the Metropolitan-Area Library Authority Act.

Sec. 2. Declaration of Policy and Purpose: Library service is an essential public service for which public funds may be expended. It is deemed to be necessary for the educational, cultural, and economic life of a metropolitan area, and for the health, safety, and welfare of its people.

It is the purpose of this Act to aid, promote, and coordinate library and information services within a metropolitan area for the benefit of all citizens residing in the area.

Sec. 3. Definitions: As used in this Act.

"Authority" means a metropolitan-area library authority:

"Metropolitan Area" means an area designated as a "standard metropolitan statistical area" by the U.S. Census Bureau, or a contiguous area of one or two counties in their entirety with a population of over 100,000;

"Board" means the Board of Directors of a metropolitan area library authority;

"Central City" means the city with the largest population in the metropolitan area;

"Central County" means the county containing the city with the largest population in the metropolitan area.

Sec. 4. Establishment of Authority: A metropolitan-area library authority shall be established upon a favorable vote of the qualified voters residing in the metropolitan area at the referendum held as provided in Section 5 of this Act. Upon its establishment the Authority shall be a unit of local government, body politic, political subdivision, and municipal corporation. It shall have the power to coordinate, facilitate, and improve library and information services in the area.

Sec. 5. Referendum on Establishment: An election to authorize the establishment of a metropolitan-area library authority may be called pursuant to a resolution adopted by the city council of the central city and the board of commissioners of each component county. The referendum election shall be conducted by the county clerk of the central county in accordance with the general election laws of the state. The question of establishing and maintaining a metropolitan area library authority shall be submitted by a separate ballot in substantially the following form:

Shall a metropolitan area library authority
be established and maintained in (name of
county or counties)? Yes. . . . No. . . .

If a majority of the persons voting on the proposition shall vote in favor thereof, the board of commissioners of the central county shall adopt a resolution setting the time and place for a meeting of the Board of Directors of the metropolitan-area library authority which shall be held not later than 30 days after the date of such election. A copy of such resolution shall be transmitted to the city council of the central city and the board of commissioners of the other component counties which are affected by the establishment of the Authority.

Sec. 6. Board of Directors: The governing body of the Authority shall be a Board of Directors consisting of nine members appointed as follows:

a) The Mayor of the central city shall appoint four members with the approval of the city council;

b) The board of commissioners of the central county shall appoint three members;

c) The board of commissioners of the other component county or counties shall appoint two members.

If the metropolitan-area library authority shall consist of only one county, the members of the Board shall be appointed as follows:

a) The Mayor of the central city shall appoint five members with the approval of the city council;

b) The board of commissioners of the central county shall appoint four members.

In making Board appointments, equal representation shall be given to public officials, librarians, and lay citizens insofar as it is practicable.

Sec. 7. Organization and Meetings: At the first meeting of the Board, the directors shall organize and elect a president and such other officers as they deem necessary. The directors shall determine the time and place of all official meetings of the Board, and shall post a notice thereof at a prominent public place within the metropolitan area one day in advance thereof.

Sec. 8. Compensation: Members of the Board shall not receive a salary nor other compensation for services as a director. However, they may be reimbursed for expenses actually incurred by them in the conduct of official business for the Authority.

Sec. 9. Powers of the Board: The Board of the Authority shall carry out the spirit and intent of this Act in coordinating, facilitating, and improving library and information services within the metropolitan area, and, in addition to but without limiting the powers conferred by this Act, shall have the following powers:

a) To make and adopt such bylaws, rules, and regulations for their own guidance and for the government of the Authority as may be expedient, not inconsistent with this Act;

b) To apply for, receive, and expend grants and other funds from the State of (name of state) or any department or agency thereof, from any unit of local government, from the federal government or any department or agency thereof, or from any other person or corporation, for use in connection with any of the powers or purposes of the Authority as set forth in this Act;

c) To make such studies as may be necessary and to enter into contracts with the State of (name of state) or any department or agency thereof, with any unit of local government, with the federal government or any department or agency thereof, or with any other person or corporation as the Board deems proper and necessary in carrying out its responsibilities as provided in this Act;

d) To purchase or lease real or personal property and to take title to any property acquired by it under the name and style of "The Board of Directors of the (name of Authority) Metropolitan-Area Library Authority";

e) To appoint a competent Executive Director and necessary assistants, to fix their compensation, to remove such appointees and to retain professional consultants as needed;

f) To sue and to be sued in the name of the Authority;

g) To sell or otherwise dispose of any real or personal property that it deems no longer necessary or useful for its purposes;

h) To invest any funds or monies not required for immediate use or disbursement;

i) To make comprehensive plans for the coordination and improvement of library and information services within the metropolitan area;

j) To accept gifts and other donations to the Authority.

Sec. 10. Annual Report: Within 90 days after the expiration of each fiscal year, the Board shall submit a written report to the state library agency. The report shall contain a) an itemized statement of the various sums of money received from all sources; and b) an itemized statement of the objects and purposes for which those sums of money have been expended. The report shall be verified under oath by the secretary or some other responsible officer of the Authority.

APPENDIX B

A MODEL LAW RELATING TO LIBRARY THEFT

Sec. 1. Declaration of Policy: Because of the rising incidence of library theft, libraries are suffering serious losses of irreplaceable books, manuscripts, and other resources. In order to preserve rare research materials for posterity, it is the policy of this state to provide libraries and their employees and agents with additional legal protection to ensure greater security for their collections.

Sec. 2. Crime of Library Theft: A person is guilty of the crime of library theft when he willfully conceals on his person or among his belongings a book or other library materials while still on the premises of the library or willfully and without authority removes a book or other library materials from such library with the intention of converting them to his own use.

Sec. 3. Presumptions: A person who willfully conceals a book or other library materials on his person or among his belongings while still on the premises of the library or in the immediate vicinity thereof shall be *prima facie* presumed to have concealed the book or other library materials with the intention of converting them to his own use. If a book or other library materials are found concealed upon his person or among his belongings, it shall be *prima facie* evidence of willful concealment.

Sec. 4. Detention: A library or an employee or agent of a library that has probable cause to believe that a person has committed library theft may detain such person on the premises of the library or in the immediate vicinity thereof for the following purposes:

a) To conduct an investigation in a reasonable manner and within a resonable length of time to determine whether such person has unlawfully concealed or removed a book or other library materials.

b) To inform a peace officer of the detention of the person and to surrender that person to the custody of a peace officer.

Sec. 5. Exemption from Liability: A library or an employee or agent of a library who detains or causes the arrest of any person pursuant to section 4 of this act shall not be held civilly or criminally liable for false arrest, false imprisonment, unlawful detention, assault, battery, slander, libel, or malicious prosecution of the person detained or arrested, provided that in detaining or causing the arrest of the person, the library or the employee or agent of the library had at the time of the detention or arrest probable cause to believe that the person committed the crime of library theft as defined in section 2 of this act.

Sec. 6. Arrest without Warrant by Peace Officer: Any peace officer may arrest without a warrant any person he has probable cause for believing has committed the crime of library theft as defined in Section 2 of this act.

Sec. 7. "Book or Other Library Materials" Defined: The terms "book or other library materials" as used in this act include any book, plate, picture, photograph, engraving, painting, drawing, map, newspaper, magazine, pamphlet, broadside, manuscript, document, letter, public record, microform, sound recording, audiovisual materials in any format, magnetic or other tapes, electronic data processing records, artifacts, or other documentary, written, or printed materials, regardless of physical form or characteristics, belong to, on loan to, or otherwise in the custody of the following: (1) any public library; (2) any library of an educational, historical or eleemosynary institution, organization. or society; (3) any museum; (4) any repository of public records.

Sec. 8. (Note: This section is reserved for the inclusion of a penalty provision for the crime of library theft, which must be fixed in accordance with the general policy of each state.)

Sec. 9. Library Theft: Construction: This act shall be construed to be cumulative and supplemental to all other laws of the state of ____________ and the crime herein defined and the presumptions herein created shall be in addition to previously existing crimes and presumptions provided by law.

Sec. 10. Copies of This Act to Be Publicly Displayed: A copy of this act shall be publicly displayed in the reading rooms of all libraries and other institutions covered by this measure.

APPENDIX C

A MODEL STATE-AID ACT IN SUPPORT OF PUBLIC LIBRARIES

Sec. 1. Since the state has a constitutional responsibility in promoting and supporting public education, and since the public library is a vital agency serving all levels of the educational process, it is hereby declared to be the policy of this state to encourage and support the improvement of free public libraries.

Sec. 2. In keeping with the above policy, provision is hereby made for a program of state financial grants designed to assist municipal governments in the maintenance and operation of free public libraries. These grants may be used for the purchase of library materials, supplies and equipment, salaries of library staff, and services. These funds may not be used for land acquisition or construction.

Sec. 3. It is hereby authorized to be appropriated for the purposes provided in Sec. 2, an amount not to exceed $1.00 per capita of the population served by each public library for the years 1982 and 1983; an amount not to exceed $2.00 per capita for the years 1984 and 1985; an amount not to exceed $3.00 per capita for the years 1986 and 1987; an amount not to exceed $4.00 per capita for the years 1988 and

1989; and an amount not to exceed $5.00 per capita for the years 1990 and 1991.

Sec. 4. The grants authorized in Sec. 3 are to be distributed by the state library agency on an equal per capita basis to all public libraries, subject to such rules and regulations as may be prescribed by the state library agency.

Sec. 5. In the event a public library receiving such grants reduces the amount of its annual tax levy or appropriation to an amount which is less than the average amount levied or appropriated for the three years immediately preceding the adoption of this act, then it shall not be eligible to receive such grants.

[*This model act, drafted by the author, is designed to implement one of the major recommendation of the report entitled* Alternatives for Financing the Public Library, *issued by the National Commission on Libraries and Information Science in 1975.*]

REFERENCES

1. *Acts and Resolves Passed by the General Court of Massachusetts* (Boston: Dutton and Wentworth, 1846), pp. 836–837.

2. *Burns Annotated Indiana Statutes*, Sec. 41-901 (Indianapolis: Bobbs-Merrill, 1975).

3. Howard Lee McBain, *American City Progress and the Law* (New York: Columbia University Press, 1918), p. 5.

4. *West's Florida Statutes Annotated*, Sec. 166.042 (St. Paul: West, 1978).

5. Carleton Bruns Joeckel, *The Government of the American Public Library* (Chicago: University of Chicago Press, 1935), p. 71.

6. *Ibid.*, p. 81.

7. William Anderson and Edward W. Weidner, *American City Government* (New York: Holt, 1950), pp. 496–497.

8. Joeckel, p. 182.

9. *Ibid.*, pp. 194–195.

10. Opinion of Evelle J. Younger, Attorney General of California, No. CV 78/96, November 21, 1978.

11. William B. Munro, *Municipal Administration* (New York: Macmillan, 1935), p. 462.

12. Joeckel, pp. 261–262.

13. *South Dakota Compiled Laws*, Sec. 14-1-40 (Indianapolis: Allen Smith, 1974).

14. P. 26.

15. Alex Ladenson, "Is the Library an Educational Institution?" *Wilson Library Bulletin*, March 1977, pp. 576–581.

16. *Consolidated Laws of New York Annotated*, Education Law, Sec. 293 (St. Paul: West, 1969).

17. *Oklahoma Statutes Annotated*, Title 65, Sec. 152 (St. Paul: West, 1964).

18. Carleton B. Joeckel, *et al.*, A *National Plan for Public Library Service* (Chicago: American Library Association, 1948), p. 18.

19. American Library Association, *Public Library Service: A Guide to Evaluation with Minimum Standards* (Chicago: American Library Association, 1956), pp. 13–14.

20. *West's Annotated California Codes*, Education Code, Sec. 18701 (St. Paul: West, 1978).

21. *Consolidated Laws of New York*, Education Code, Sec. 272, Par. 2a (St. Paul: West, 1978).

22. *Ibid.*, Par. 2g.

23. *Smith-Hurd Illinois Annotated Statutes*, Chap. 128, Sec. 107 (St. Paul: West, 1978).

24. Alex Ladenson, "The Metropolitan Area Library Authority: A New Structure for Service, *Library Journal*, November 15, 1974, pp. 2395–2398.

25. *Nevada Revised Statutes*, Sec. 385.240 (Carson City: Legislative Council Bureau, 1979).

26. *West's Florida Statutes Annotated*, Sec. 233.65 (St. Paul: West, 1978).

27. *University of Illinois Statutes*, July 18, 1979, pp. 24–25.

28. Clark Byse and Louis Goughin, *Tenure in American Higher Education* (Ithaca: Cornell University Press, 1959).

29. *General Revision of the Copyright Law,* Title 17 of the United States Code, House-Senate Conference Report, No. 94-1733, pp. 72–73.

30. *Copyright Law Revision*, House Report, No. 94-1476, pp. 68–70.

31. *Federal Register,* November 6, 1977, p. 59265.

32. Alex Ladenson, "Library Security and the Law," *College & Research Libraries,* March 1977, pp. 109–117.

INDEX